From Dysfunction to Innovation in Technology

From Dysfunction to Innovation in Technology

Overcoming Critical Infrastructure and Organizational Dynamics in Education

Darryl Vidal

ROWMAN & LITTLEFIELD
Lanham • Boulder • New York • London

Published by Rowman & Littlefield
An imprint of The Rowman & Littlefield Publishing Group, Inc.
4501 Forbes Boulevard, Suite 200, Lanham, Maryland 20706
www.rowman.com

6 Tinworth Street, London SE11 5AL, United Kingdom

Copyright © 2020 by Darryl Vidal

All rights reserved. No part of this book may be reproduced in any form or by any electronic or mechanical means, including information storage and retrieval systems, without written permission from the publisher, except by a reviewer who may quote passages in a review.

British Library Cataloguing in Publication Information Available

Library of Congress Cataloging-in-Publication Data

ISBN 9781475848939 (cloth)
ISBN 9781475848946 (pbk.)
ISBN 9781475848953 (electronic)

Contents

Acknowledgments	ix
Preface	xi
Introduction: How to Take Your School from Ed Tech Dysfunction to Ed Tech Innovation	1
Chapter 1 Disrupting Education Technology	5
Strategic Planning and Vision	5
Ed Tech and IT in the District Organizational Chart	11
Assess Your School's Technology Integration	14
Status Quo	19
The SAMR Model	20
The Leapfrog Effect	24
Disruption	25
SAMR Disruption	25
Chapter 1—Action Items	26
Chapter 2 Instructional and Technological Innovation Strategy	29
Below the Line of Discontent	31
Moving above the Line of Discontent	34
Ed Tech Status Quo and Innovation	45
IT Status Quo	46
Challenging Past Practices and Legacy Procedures	46
Chapter 2—Action Items	48
Chapter 3 Key Technology Systems/Features	49
Learning Management Systems	49
Collaboration	58

Content Development Platform	64
Standards for Development	67
Chapter 3—Action Items	67
Chapter 4 A New Name for Redefinition	**69**
Tier 4 Curriculum—The 6Cs	74
Development Resources	77
Chapter 4—Action Items	78
Chapter 5 The 6C Development Process	**81**
Curriculum	81
Core	81
Cognitive Factors	82
Context	84
Critical Thinking	85
Collaboration	87
The 6C Survey Form for T4c Development	88
Artifacts—What Are the Resultant T4c Components?	89
Chapter 5—Action Items	91
Chapter 6 What's after the 6Cs?	**93**
Implementation	93
Assessment	95
Evaluation	100
Design versus Development	102
Who	104
What	104
When	104
Chapter 6—Action Items	106
Chapter 7 Disrupting Incremental Innovation	**107**
Advocacy	107
Organic Growth	108
Pilot Projects	108
Clearinghouse	109
Site-Wide Initiatives	110
Grade-level Initiatives	110
District-Wide Initiatives	110

State-Wide Initiatives	111
Strategies for Implementation and Deployment—Creating a T4c Development Team	111
What Are the Qualifications and Experience Necessary to Be on the T4c Development Team?	113
Work Request Process	117
Chapter 7—Action Items	120
Chapter 8 Full-Scale T4c Deployment	**123**
Technology Skills	123
Possible Negative Impacts of Collaboration	126
Teacher Functional Knowledge	127
Professional Development	130
Chapter 8—Action Items	133
Moving Forward	133
References	**137**
About the Author	**139**

Acknowledgments

From Dysfunction to Innovation in Technology is my most ambitious book on education technology to date. Although I know my VISION is on track based on my most recent experience and technology projects, the idea that I can have an impact on all technology-enabled curriculum is hopeful at best.

I don't know where I would be without my beloved wife to always keep me grounded by asking the always important questions, such as who is going to read this book? And why?

Without this most relevant of curiosities, my imagination might run wild and away from reality. So I dedicate this most ambitious of books to my family: wife April, sons Justin and Bradley, daughters Shaina and Nissa-Belle, without whom I would truly lack perspective.

I also include an additional acknowledgment to my eldest daughter Shaina, now a third-grade teacher, who has helped review and provide some insight into the challenges of teaching in today's new world of education technology.

Preface

Having consulted for K–12 school districts for over twenty years, I've seen technology take its place and evolve from a nascent promise to be all things to all people to becoming a burden and a distraction to finally, today, taking its place as the tool that will take today's curriculum to the next level.

We can look today and see wonderful examples of highly interactive and engaging lesson plans that foster critical thinking and collaboration, but have we seen true examples of district-wide mass production of highly interactive and collaborative curriculum made available to all teachers? And shall we assume that the critical success factor for this type of curriculum might be infrastructure, teachers with requisite skills, and professional development that ensures the correct application of said curriculum?

For some of these solutions, K–12 education can look to higher education for the clues. Many, if not all, institutions of higher learning have adopted and achieved this advanced level of curriculum and practicum. Online learning 13-20 has successfully embraced the capabilities that technology offers in communication, control, sharing, collaboration, and so on. Tools such as Blackboard and Google Classroom have seen wide-scale adoption and standardized implementation in colleges and universities. So why is K–12 a step behind?

This book will not only answer this question, it will also provide the roadmap to the solution, a roadmap that will allow you (yes, you!) to become the champion of advanced curriculum development for your school/district and achieve the promise of technology in the classroom.

The SAMR model (substitution, augmentation, modification, and redefinition), as originally described and popularized by Dr. Ruben Puentedura, introduced the concept of redefining curriculum to optimize and leverage technology and then applying this technology in more advanced methods through an incremental adoption and implementation process. But with all the discussion and innovation around the progression, no one has asked the question: why take these steps incrementally? Until now.

That's where the concept of disruption comes into play. There is no need to step up the ladder defined by SAMR. Just start at the top tier, what I've designated Tier 4 curriculum (T4c).

This book will tell you how to do this in a detailed, step-by-step process. By using the success of online learning implemented in higher education as a guide, this book lays out the process using the 6C process of defining and developing T4c in a way that makes it easy to implement and train teachers in its use. Better still, T4c provides the teacher flexibility to affect and implement the curriculum to best suit each individual class and delivery method.

So, buckle up and get ready because when you're done reading this, there will be no reason not to start your school's T4c development initiative.

Introduction

How to Take Your School from Ed Tech Dysfunction to Ed Tech Innovation

Education has been forever impacted by technology. Just like the Beatles in the 1960s, once rock and roll came into the picture, the music industry and society felt a tremendous impact that touched every aspect of our daily lives. Even more so with technology than with the Beatles, the world around us changed in a matter of months and years instead of decades or generations.

People walking around with Bluetooth earbuds, and cell phone watches have made technology devices more invisible and ubiquitous. Soon devices will be implanted in our clothes, under our skin, and eventually in our brains: are today's educators comfortable with that idea?

Adults growing up in the 1960s, 1970s, and 1980s often talk about being digital immigrants and the children of their generation being digital natives, but this premise has changed as even millennials (born in the 1990s) talk about being unable to keep pace with technology.

As such, the integration and assimilation of technology into the instructional environment lagged in the early stages, but now that the network physical layer and systems infrastructures are well understood and almost as well funded, educators have seen a plethora of technology propagated throughout schools. The question then becomes this: have curriculum and learning management systems manifested to truly improve education at a community, state, or nationwide level?

This book deals with the concept of the SAMR model—don't worry, we'll cover it in depth—but the point is to go past the model. Because the model, in and of itself, simply presents a challenge with little guidance—a goal without clear direction to achieve it.

It's a statement of fact, wherein some schools and districts find themselves somewhere in the spectrum of the model—maybe low, maybe high—but the model doesn't provide instructions on how to move up the spectrum. As individual teachers, they can only look to a district resource to help achieve the objectives they may define on their own as they recognize the challenge of SAMR.

The concept of disruption will also be tackled in this book, but the main point of this book is what the author has designated Tier 4 curriculum—or T4c. This book is about how to take your school past the progression of the SAMR model, how to jump past GO, collect $200, and move directly to T4c.

Like politics, all education is local. How do educational trends and tools affect the students around you and your community? It is almost irrelevant what is happening at a federal or state level. How districts and superintendents decide to focus on and implement these technologies and the curriculum is the salient factor. What are the metrics to pursue, the models to implement? And how?

Schools and school districts are vastly different from each other. Everything from geography, demographics, socioeconomic status, cultural aspects, and student-racial diversity create a unique school with unique needs.

The concept of disruption is nothing new, however, the application and process for affecting disruption is as unique as each individual school and district. Because of this codified individuality, it will never make good general sense for one school or district to copy another.

This uniqueness negates the significance of general-purpose technology. That's not to say that every school could benefit from upgraded technology infrastructure and classroom technology, but we're now at a place in time where these are mostly given. Today's schools are designed with wireless saturation, LANs, WANs, and Internet. Most classrooms now have interactive televisions (some have old projectors) and student devices.

Educators have seen that the presence of these technologies and devices don't automatically yield benefits—and in some cases, quite the opposite. The schools that have defined and implemented technology professional development, mentoring, and coaching models have been the most successful at implementing technology-based curriculum at a higher percentage of classrooms and teachers, but until the baby boomers are completely retired, we're sure there will be some hold-outs for another decade or so.

This common denominator of infrastructure and software is just step 1. What is step 2, 3, and 4? There must be a plan, and fortunately, one trend of online learning and technology application in higher education has laid out a plan. Not yet discreet and documented for application by K–12 districts, but the means and guidance is there for those who are looking.

Having recently (2017) completed an MA Ed. in instructional technology at Cal State, the author was fortunate enough to get his fill of every professor's flavor of technology, from some of the foremost instructional technology development faculty to the opposite side of the spectrum.

By experiencing firsthand the perspective of a technology implementation consultant for K–12 schools, the author can detail the pathway forward. But it's not a simple step up the ladder. Educators and administrators have to be prepared for a giant leap forward, engaging community, funding, and mindsharing throughout the process.

The endeavor must be endorsed and advocated from the top, meaning that this indoctrination must start with school superintendents who are ready to commit resources to the endeavor, as long as someone can define clearly the objectives and deliverables of this endeavor.

So, who can determine the needs and lay out the plan? It will rarely be one person. It must be a team, a team lead by vision and leadership, provided with plans and resources. This book will take an in-depth look into the technology infrastructure and vision required to bring a school district to this pinnacle, and to also acknowledge that it is a path of constant change and revision. Each year new strategies and tactics will be required to achieve the ever-changing vision for each school.

Beyond technology and infrastructure there's so much more. In fact, technology and infrastructure are requisite, but the ultimate objective of T4c is entirely dependent on nontechnological factors: vision, leadership, resources, standards, training/mentoring, and professional development. It is also true that without a specific objective and plan to develop T4c, the technology and infrastructure will benefit some, not all, and may cause mass confusion and chaos for others.

It is always better to grab the bull by the horns than to let it run wild on its own, but the ride will be a wild one.

Chapter 1

Disrupting Education Technology

STRATEGIC PLANNING AND VISION

In previous books, *Vision* (2014) and *Fail to Plan, Plan to Fail* (2017), the author did a deep dive into how to document a vision for a school and/or district, and then how to turn that vision into a strategic plan. What makes a strategic plan actionable? Two things: an implementation plan and money. The implementation plans must lay out projects, resources, start and end dates, tasks, sequences, and dependencies. The money enables the engagement of resources and the procurement of materials, licenses, contracts, and services.

Without these, school districts and organizations will languish in chaos, where confusion and dissension reign, where personalities and fiefdoms pervade, and where status quo takes an organization backward relative to the rest of the industry because that organization is not moving forward. School superintendents see districts around them moving forward with technology initiatives and feel left out—without a plan—in essence, standing still while other schools trudge forward.

What makes an LCAP (local control and accountability plan) or mission statement actionable? For education technology, it is the technology design and implementation plan, but what form does this plan take?

The process of defining the initiatives of a strategic plan and turning them into discrete project plans is called *project planning*. Project plans must be specific in scope, time, and budget. Scope must be specific in terms of systems, technologies, parts, and execution.

Time must be specific to resource and site availability. Budget must encompass all aspects of planning and implementation, including consulting, and training. My last book, *Project Management in the Ed Tech Era* (2018) takes the reader to the next step through tactical planning and implementation. The MAPIT® project planning process defined in it can make any school more effective both strategically and tactically.

This book will attempt to bridge the gap between vision and implementation, but more importantly, understand the ultimate objective of the

SAMR promise, and take strides that can achieve the highest-level goals and objectives. Why shoot for the clouds when you can shoot for the stars?

The concept and exercise of developing a vision is more than just words on a web page, it consists of actionable strategic plans, initiatives, and tactical plans that support the objective. But beyond that even, the idea of ed tech systems and practicum becomes an operational initiative. How can educators plan, implement, model, train, and maintain these concepts and systems?

This question assumes that leadership understands the concept of turning vision into reality, using budgets, edicts, and models. It is not just enough to say, "This is where we want to go." Leadership must find the answers to these questions:

1. What are the initiatives that will get us there?
2. What systems must be in place to achieve this end?
3. What infrastructure must be in place to support the systems?
4. What kind of instructional personnel must be in place to develop the models for these initiatives?
5. What tools will be required to support district-wide access to these systems?
6. What training and professional development (PD) models are required to indoctrinate the teachers?

Take an initial stab at answering these questions, and these might be the responses:

1. What are the initiatives that will get us there?

These initiatives must focus on LCAP and board objectives, but they must also be definable and executable. Beyond that, there must be commitment from leadership and administration to engage and task the resources to define and plan these initiatives, and then carry the initiatives from strategy to tactics. Not only must dollars be allocated to these initiatives, but human resources must be dedicated and guided to these ends. But what does this convoluted sentence really mean?

Leadership must identify staff (resources) and dedicate a portion of their time to define and plan the key technology initiatives for the near-term (say twelve to twenty-four months). Then they must engage (pay for) resources to implement these plans (buy and install stuff).

It's not enough to tell the TOSAs (teachers on special assignment), "We want to do this." They must be told, "We want to do this, this way, using these tools, in this standard method, to achieve these standards, in this time frame."

And who are these people who will do this—who can do this? It's not the superintendent, or even the assistant superintendent of instruction. They are the leadership, but the vision and guidance must be provided by leadership to dictate to the coordinators and TOSAs the who, what, when, where, and how of these initiatives.

These initiatives don't stand alone. They are dependent on each other. First comes infrastructure, then implementation of systems, then the modeling of use, and the development of curriculum, then the development of training, then the actual training, and then evaluation, refinement, redefinition, more modeling, more development of training, then more training—and the cycle continues.

2. What systems must be in place to achieve this end?

This is a complicated question. It's likely that the superintendent or assistant superintendent don't know the answer to these questions either. As much as they want to implement curriculum that achieves Common Core objectives, requires critical thinking, group work, and collaboration, the actual software applications can vary and be dynamic year to year. What is best implemented using Blackboard one year may be better suited to Google Classroom in year two, and you name the next LMS (learning management system) that will be *en vogue* in the succeeding years.

Like the previous decade when technology educators anguished over the Mac, iPad, or PC question, assuming these debates have been settled and school technology has matured to the point that all schools can support all platforms as required by curriculum, schools can attempt to define what systems should be invested in, for what time frame, and to achieve what objectives.

Like any other technology question, there will *not* be one ultimate system that will work for all schools, all teachers, and all students, in all demographics. So, who will stick this stake in the ground? Guess what, superintendent? It's you again, putting your reputation and political capital at risk to implement the systems defined, designed, and recommended by . . . whom?

3. What infrastructure must be in place to support the systems?

Think of the amount of infrastructure put in place simply because it was the trend. In the early 2000s, many very large districts began developing standards for fiber to the classroom. The basis for this design seemed sound—at the time. Leadership wanted to install infrastructure that would enable the maximum bandwidth for technology systems seven to ten years into the future. At the time, maximum bandwidth was fiber-based, so this was not a bad assumption.

Through the years, fiber has and continues to support higher bandwidths than copper cabling. However, the equipment, both from the horizontal distribution and the endpoints (computers) did not use this medium.

Instead, manufacturers pushed the bandwidth capabilities of copper well beyond what was previously publicized. Instead of endpoints adopting fiber-based interfaces, they simply took advantage of new bandwidths achieved through Category 5, 5e, and then on to 6 pushing the bandwidths from 1 Mpbs, to 10 Mbps, and up to 1 Gbps, and yes to 10 Gbps—all on copper. So what happened to the fiber in the classroom?

This standard led to millions of dollars in fiber infrastructure that couldn't be utilized in the out years because copper continued to push the standard for horizontal distribution. Think of cable plants, and fiber installation, installed but never used because the network switches were copper based. The fiber to the classroom was easily a multi-billion-dollar boondoggle that many local taxpayers are still paying for through bond modernization programs in years ten to thirty—let's not add it up.

We can recall doing an assessment for another school district that did the same thing—fiber to each classroom. This one included multiple fiber drops in each classroom. No equipment was ever connected to those fibers. After year one, many of the terminations were broken off by students brushing their chairs and backpacks against the wall. The fiber was rendered useless within that first year, but that didn't matter.

This is only one example of misdirected funding for infrastructure. Consider the thousands of iPads and laptops purchased using thirty-year bonds. These devices rarely achieved either their expected use or lifespan. Many even weren't used effectively in their debuts, and some were used as platforms for attack on the district infrastructure. Students learned to hack iPads faster than the district learned to secure them.

Having had this sobering experience, how can such misapplications of technology be averted in the future? These days the standard of schools infrastructure consists of wired and wireless infrastructure that can support upward of fifty to ninety devices in each classroom, mobile device management (MDM), 1 to 10 Gbps wide area networks (WANs) supporting high-bandwidth connectivity between sites and the Internet service provider (ISP), and cloud-based computing, storage, backup, and disaster recovery. It doesn't even sound cheap, but the good news is many districts have stepped up and implemented this base-level infrastructure to take the next step.

4. What kind of instructional personnel must be in place to develop the models for these initiatives?

This question becomes even more complex. How can instructional support coordinators and TOSAs, define curriculum (grade level) to achieve these objectives without first being fully indoctrinated into the tools and methods?

This is not a one-week training, off-site or in-service. We're talking about objective-driven training in curriculum development, instructional design, and a specific suite of technology tools that will be available to the teachers for whom they will be developing.

These are those tech teachers, early adopters, and instructional standouts that now must be taken out of their classrooms and given the task of defining standards, and then developing curriculum that will achieve these objectives. What are the objectives again? Critical thinking exercises, collaboration, group work and—oh yeah—Common Core. But once again, who defines the models? Is it these resources?

No, it's the manufacturers and developers of these platforms. The teachers and coordinators don't go to Google or Blackboard and say, "This is how we imagine using technology." It's the other way around. Coordinators and instructional superintendents look at the different platforms available and then say, "Yes, we want to adopt the methods defined by this manufacturer/developer." Is this really the right way to define systems?

5. What platforms will be required to support district-wide access to these systems?

Here's a great chicken-and-egg question: Who will decide on these platforms? The coordinators and TOSAs? Or will these platforms be defined as standards in their planning, development, and implementation? Sounds scary right? Will leadership determine the platforms or the other way around? Knowing that left to their own devices, teachers will do whatever is necessary to achieve their daily teaching requirements—meaning that they typically are focused on daily lessons and classroom management—not district-wide or even site-wide initiatives.

Tech teachers and tech TOSAs typically do a lot of their own research and development. This means that their efforts are *not* driven by standards of platform and development. Once these resources are taken out of their classroom and tasked with defining platforms, standards, and curriculum development methods for their teaching brethren, who oversees and validates their work? And more importantly, how does this model scale?

6. What standards need to be established?

Standards are both guidelines and constraints. Their benefit is arguable in individual instances, but for the most part, standards for curriculum development aren't a bad thing. The question becomes "Where do these standards come from?" and "To what extent can these standards be enforced?" The good news is that when presented under a positive light, standards are accepted and adhered to. If they are left to their own, then it's easy to see a lack of adherence to these unenforced standards accompanied by a lack of cohesion and centralized planning.

The answer is it's not the information technology (IT) department's responsibility to address standards for educational technology and curriculum. It is their responsibility to adhere to, and comply with, industry standards and IT infrastructure standards and best practices. There is no need in education today to reinvent the IT wheel.

The IT department doesn't want to look like it's dictating the learning process but rather that it is enhancing the learning construct for all users. Besides, who said IT has anything to do with instructional guidelines for curriculum development?

7. What processes are required to enable content development?

What is this question even about? What processes? Let us explain. A district with a T4c content development team will invariably receive a bounty of content requests. Every discipline and every grade level will ask for their content to be prioritized. What will be the submission requirement? How much content will be provided to the team versus developed by the team? Who will decide?

We can see from this line of questioning that once a district develops resources for centralized curriculum development and instructional design—a process or survey questionnaire will be required to get compulsory data and information from the requestor in a standardized format. The good news is that this book will provide this survey form. It's called the T4c development template.

8. Who will develop content? Site or district resources?

Without a T4c development team, who else might a school or district ask to develop? Why not each individual teacher? Isn't this model scalable? Yes, it is scalable. Each teacher developing content will be the subject matter expert (SME) as well as the content developer and the instructional designer. Doesn't sound like a lofty plan, does it?

9. Who are the subject matter experts (SMEs)?

Everyone or no one? Paid or unpaid? Site or district? Credentials?

10. What training and PD models are required to help get the teachers up to speed?

Assuming these methods, platforms, and standards are identified and developed, what PD and training programs will support implementation throughout classrooms? It is easy to agree that the annual in-service training is not enough. In fact, it's not even close. This is where a variety of models for training, coaching, mentoring, training trainers, and paying vendors still falls short. Yet there are no easy answers. So instead of identifying all the challenges and difficulties, let's get on to solutions.

ED TECH AND IT IN THE DISTRICT ORGANIZATIONAL CHART

In the books *N3XT Practices* (Vidal and Casey 2014) and *Vision* (Vidal and Casey 2014), the authors wrote extensively about ed tech and IT in the organizational structure. In fact, those books—written circa 2014—compared various organizational structures where the IT department reported to business or instruction and even discussed the need for the CIO/CTO position (chief information officer/chief technology officer).

These analyses weren't off base, but in 2020 the technology platforms supporting education have become so complex and ubiquitous they require true engineering skill sets to plan, implement, and maintain—there is no educational skill set required to maintain and support these technology platforms. Networks, servers (physical or virtual/public or private cloud), Wi-Fi, and WANs don't need any teaching expertise in their maintenance and support—they need real system and network engineers.

Educational systems such as student information, learning management and decision support systems are complex database systems. Teachers must be trained in their use in the classroom to support learning objectives, but teachers don't need to know what, where, or how these systems are managed and maintained—the systems just need to work.

What's the implication of such a premise? Well first, there would be no concept of a CTO, CIO, or assistant superintendent of IT, or even a tech TOSA. Sorry to say that these technical leaders only ensure that tech bias *is* injected into everything, when the opposite should be the case. That's not to say that the IT department goes away, but the idea of an ed tech department does go away. Consider that school districts don't have a plumbing technology department or an electrical technology department. These are infrastructure systems that are necessary for operations but not as an educational focus. This concept relegates the

IT department to becoming a maintenance and support organization for technology infrastructure just like the facilities and maintenance and operations departments support and maintain the plumbing and electrical systems.

In their book *Vision* (2014), the authors examined the implications of the IT department within the district organization. Many IT directors and technologists believe that schools need a CTO or CIO. But in *Vision*, they debunk this concept. There is no need for these positions because they will only ensure that initiatives are focused on technology as opposed to learning and instruction.

Can you imagine a CIO saying, "It's not about the technology, it's about the instructional practice." No—for a CTO or CIO, it will always be about the technology, and the superintendent that has this position within their organization will fight this concept at the cabinet level.

The author relates a story where he once was told by an IT director that any staff with "technology" in their title should report to the IT director. Doesn't that concept seem fundamentally wrong? The author's response was that no position in instructional services should have technology in their title. Sorry for all the balloons this assertion has just burst, but how are the network and servers any different than air-conditioning and electricity?

Classrooms can't operate without these, but there is no chief air-conditioning officer. To take the idea one step further, think of who in the organization would advocate for a CIO (or CTO)? Of course, it's the IT director, because he (or she) has topped out! The author has always joked that CIO stands for "Career Is Over"! What do they have to do with students and learning? Our typical response?

We always advise superintendents that he or she wouldn't want the tech guy (or girl) in cabinet. They are not instructional experts. In fact, teachers that ascend to IT director typically don't have the engineering background to truly understand the fundamentals of the systems they are designing and managing. So, they typically hire IT resources who are engineers, and then try to manage them as if they understood these systems—when they really don't.

How can modern school districts address technology implementation without injecting a technology bias into the organization? Meaning—instead of having "technology" resources for instruction, all instructional models and staff are technology empowered, capable, and/or cognizant—not technology focused—but the lesson plan leverages technology capabilities.

In fact, instead of having instructional technology staff, there should only be instructional support staff for the curricular platforms. Instead of having an ed tech resource, the STEM (science, technology, engineering, and math), ELA (English language arts), and VAPA (visual and performing arts) resources synthesize technology into the implementation—they are all ed tech experts, but none with a specific technology focus.

Then the instructional support staff only needs to focus on curriculum and models—forget about technology; it's already there. Or at least it should be. It does make perfect sense for the instructional services department to have an LMS resource, a data and analytics (D&A) resource and an SIS (student information service) resource—but clearly, their focus would be on instructional application of these platforms—these are not database analysts or programmers—they are coordinators and TOSAs focused not on the technology but on the classroom use models.

Just as a STEM curriculum doesn't focus on STEM—the STEM emphasis is synthesized through the curriculum—technology is no longer the focus but a tool to be synthesized to support critical thinking and collaboration models. However, the technology suite is many times more complex than the textbook and workbook.

All the pieces must work together simultaneously to support each individual student and device doing a variety of activities, each putting a separate load on; device, Wi-Fi, LAN, WAN, core, and ISP. Extend that model to the cloud services and it becomes glaringly clear that this web of tech stuff must all be planned, provisioned, implemented, and supported in order to support the day-to-day needs of the classroom teacher (all of them).

This is like having the district plumber and facilities director define instruction. IT systems are not much different than plumbing and electrical power. They are essential to the operation of the school, but they just need to work, no one cares who makes the faucets and transformers just as long as they wet whistles and run computers and air-conditioning.

In fact, herein lies a conflict. The organizational structure and the departmental leaders are pitted in a complex dance over control and customer service. Many school districts suffer from dysfunction within their organizations and between their organizations. Instructional objectives of flexibility and access to all modes and media conflicts with technology focus on standards, security, and systems management. It goes back to the old IT adage that an organization either has a well-managed network or happy users—never both.

As the teachers need access to a plethora of unsecured instructional websites, IT directors want to white-list acceptable websites and relegate teachers to using only resources that have been approved by—whom? The IT director. Go ahead and think about how much sense this makes.

ASSESS YOUR SCHOOL'S TECHNOLOGY INTEGRATION

In order to assess and analyze the current state of educational technology at your school district, look at baseline metrics to establish a starting point. Table 1.1 details an objective summary of instructional and technological review relative to "industry standards" or within the educational realm and educational trends.

The table defines three-levels of technology integration within any school: Low-level integration that almost every school has, medium-level integration that most schools have, and high-level integration that only some schools have. Review the table to see where your school or district's technology integration level is currently.

This table is not exhaustive, but each school can easily be classified within these levels of integration. At the highest level of integration, schools should have these types of features and capabilities.

Communications Platforms

Communication platforms support two types of communication—messaging between users and presentation to users. This includes the electronic mail system and software like Google Hangouts or even PowerPoint that enhance a user's ability to communicate with others. These platforms have been around much longer and are more traditional and sequential.

E-mail is still the lowest common denominator for basic communications and sharing of data. Fundamentally, it's the least efficient form, requiring servers and mail servers based on domains. Sharing of files is basically sending a copy of a file instead of syncing or sharing a single file on a collaboration platform. The issue that arises from these rudimentary communications platforms is the proliferation of multiple copies of files. If you send a homework file to your teacher, who then marks it up and sends it back, you now have two separate files to manage.

Multiply this operation by 150 students and the file management aspect of this platform easily becomes unmanageable. Thus, the most basic e-mail platforms like MS Exchange/Office and Google Mail (Gmail) continue to be prevalent for these types of communications, but much of these capabilities have been replaced in the classroom with much more efficient and effective platforms for messaging and sharing documents.

Collaboration Platforms

Collaboration platforms are a step beyond basic communications and include the sharing and networking applications that allow students to work with each other, share ideas and notes, and collaborate on projects

Table 1.1. Educational Technology Trends—Circa 2019

Technology	All Schools	Most Schools	Some Schools
Network/Internet	Wi-Fi, LANs, WAN, Internet	Wi-Fi saturation within buildings	Redundancy, cloud, full-mobility campus-wide
Classroom Technology	Teacher computer, projector/display	+ Document camera, audio enhancement, interactive display	+ Makerspace, tech pod, video production, 3-D printer
Student Devices	Classroom set	Student tablet/Chromebook	Student laptop device compatibility
Site Media	Library/media center	Makerspace, robotics, coding lab, video production studio	< in multiple classrooms
Learning Management	Basic suite, productivity training	SIS integration, annual training	Full LMS feature set with district PD, coaching/mentoring
Collaboration Platform	Skype-type	Multiuser	Multimodal
Content Development Instructional Design	None	District- or some site-based development, district standards	District-based content development team
Data Analytics	None/Basic	State standards comparison, district/site	Access to D&A via student web portal
Web and Portal Services	Basic website	Web portal student assessment data, security	Full integration with student assessment data, security, pathways

and homework in real time (synchronously). Applications that support collaborative work and sharing such as wikis, Edmodo, and VoiceThread are common examples in K–12 education. Collaboration, different from communications, is much more efficient and effective for the classroom/teacher and student's scenario.

By supporting messaging, chat, conferencing, and document sharing, the options for implementing collaboration models is unlimited. For instance, a lesson plan might be implemented in one session as an individual student-based lesson while the teacher is becoming more familiar with the curriculum and how the students assimilate the cognitive factors of the lesson (more on this later).

As the teacher gains better understanding of how to implement the lesson plan leveraging the collaboration platforms, the teacher can first adapt the lesson plan delivery to utilize the distribution and sharing aspects of the collaboration platform. As the teacher begins to implement more complex group work scenarios, the teacher can require group work, sharing, and messaging as a basis for assessment and discussion, and performance models for advanced-level delivery of homework and group work.

Content Development and Sharing

Today's flexible curriculum models are primarily centered around content and the development of content—in addition to providing a standardized LMS platform—must support a multitude of communication and collaboration models around that content.

Teachers and their PD models must embrace and support planning, research, and development of customized content based on the grade-level curriculum adopted by the district and in alignment with state standards. The content development platform must also provide categorical reference and searchability of any content delivered within the school's curricular universe.

This type of state-of-the-development platform would require extensive internal resources for curriculum development, instructional design and custom LMS or web-based development. On the technology side, this highest level would extend all reported data to the students and parents, and as applicable, to the community at large.

Robotics, Makerspaces, and Coding

Instructional trends include hands-on, interactive, and group-work models. Customized spaces within classrooms or media centers allow small groups to actually create machines and devices that challenge all aspects of STEM and advanced instructional models and modules. Table 1.2 details specific instructional trends in the classroom space.

Each of these specific areas are diverse in focus and infrastructure requirements. It would be reasonable to assert that each site should have these platforms although a standardized investment in each of the

Table 1.2. Instructional Trends in the Classroom

Instructional Trends	Facilities and Infrastructure Requirements
Robotics	Robotics curriculum typically consists of robotics kits that can be purchased for grade-level and complexity. These kits can be used in most classrooms that support hands-on group work, and pod-type collaboration scenarios. Robotics initiatives can take the form of a maker "space," a kit for each classroom (grade level), a summer camp, a classroom focus or theme, or even a competition team. Coding opportunities are embedded in robotics through the use of programmable interfaces.
Makerspaces	A makerspace is a collaborative workspace within a school, library, or separate public/private facility for creating, learning, exploring, and sharing using high-tech and no tech tools. These spaces are open to students and have a variety of equipment including 3-D printers, laser cutters, CNC machines, soldering irons, and even sewing machines. However, a makerspace does not have to include all of these machines, or even any of them, to be considered a makerspace. A dedicated space that has cardboard, scissors, Lego-type construction kits and art supplies, can be a makerspace. It is more about the mindset of the participants to create something out of nothing and to explore their own interests, which make up the core of the makerspace concept. These rooms help prepare those who need the critical skills of the twenty-first century in science, technology, engineering, and math (STEM). They offer hand-in-hand learning, help with critical thinking skills, and increased self-esteem. Some of the skills learned in a makerspace include electronics, 3-D printing, 3-D modeling, coding, robotics, and even woodworking. Makerspaces also promote entrepreneurship and are used as incubators and accelerators for business start-ups.
Coding	Coding is the introduction to computer programming or coding to elementary school students. Other instructional platforms such as robotics and makerspaces may also consist of programming to control the robots or the production of audio, video, and multimedia presentations. Website coding can consist of HTML and Wordpress or a plethora of other development platforms. Coding is fully in alignment with STEM focus; however, the question must be asked, do all students need to learn to code? The argument cannot be made that all people in business or trades must know how to code, but the logic and problem-solving element of coding does warrant some early-stage exposure to uncover latent talents and interest.

library/media centers could be a focus for developing customized spaces for these areas at each school or at STEM-focused schools.

Educational Technology Proficiency

Many districts have requirements for basic technology proficiency for teachers and staff. Most county or state offices of education offer many technology learning programs and resources, but often these "attend if you can" type offerings are difficult to allocate paid-time-off to support.

These basic skills using the teacher's device of choice (whether it be Windows, Mac, or Chromebook based), accessing the Internet and other digital services, and proficiency with MS Office or the Google Apps suite of applications should include mail, word processing, spreadsheets, presentation, and at least one other graphics manipulation and creation package.

Data Integration and Reporting

Data integration is the combining of data from two or more disparate systems to create new data types and inform district instruction as well as state and government entities of the state of affairs in student achievement and demographic data not available from these disparate systems. For instance, chronic absenteeism and its impact on student achievement require the comingling of data between student information and gradebook applications.

Although the data exists in these systems, accessing and reporting this data requires sophisticated data warehousing applications, or custom integration using application programming interfaces. At more advanced levels of data analytics and reporting, teachers would have real-time access to attendance and assessment data in order to inform teachers and staff of daily performance for classroom management and planning.

Administration would have dashboards that display real-time attendance and student achievement data that would allow better communications between administration and staff. Departments like transportation and human resources would have daily or even hourly updates for student location or emergency contact information.

Web and Portal Services

A common district goal is to increase parent and community engagement. The school's web portal becomes the center-point for *all* high-level data integration and analytics. Since its importance becomes elevated with each additional value-add, the fundamental capacity to customize web pages and integrate data becomes the basis for offering relevant, and up-to-date information for all interest groups.

Table 1.3. Web and Portal Services Interest Groups

Students & Parents	Staff & Administration	City Government	Business & Community
E-mail	Schedule	School District Maps &	Business/School Partnerships
Homework (LMS)	Students	School Maps	Education Nonprofits
Grades	Gradebook	City & District Programs	Career & Vocational Training
Attendance	Assessments		School to Work
Lunch	LMS & Curriculum		
Schedule	Electronic Learning Resources		
Assessments	Analytics & Decision Support		
Pathways			

STATUS QUO

The notion of status quo, or *the current state of things*, in the realm of technology can also be viewed as a concept of standing still—or not falling down, but also not moving forward. The technology realm is guided by Moore's Law that states, "Overall processing power will double every two years."

This exponential expansion when applied to schools and school district manifests in infrastructure requirements and device counts growing in the thousands of percentiles—imagine the growth of moving from one computer per staff member to one computer per student, and the impact on wireless and wired network capacity.

If organizations are not advancing at the pace of technological growth, they are losing ground to the rest of the community at that same rate. Worse yet, if obsolescence or dysfunction of any sort become part of the infrastructure or organizational environment (ed tech and IT), the status quo is not.

Some of these characteristics can be observed in a school district's inability to report data effectively—both internally (e.g., chronic absenteeism) and externally (e.g., student achievement data), respond efficiently and effectively to projects and requests, develop customized and integrated reports and dashboards, and foster a cohesive strategic cooperation between instruction and IT operations.

The author's previous books have taken detailed looks at strategic planning and project management for education technology. These subject areas tend to focus on infrastructure systems, which in turn, are IT focused. As education technology has matured and infrastructure has been better understood and implemented, the technologist can now focus attention and take a detailed look at the instructional side of education technology.

As always, the educator must focus on objectives. Just as technology and infrastructure should never be the focus of instruction, similarly, instructional systems and their associated applications should never be the focus—except for those few responsible for planning, implementing, and maintaining these instructional systems.

Now that we're in our second generation of classroom technology standards (let's say ceiling-mounted projectors and teacher laptops as first generation, and interactive displays, student devices, and LMSs as second generation), a school can tackle the more instruction-focused aspects of curriculum and curriculum development.

Just because a teacher now has a second-generation classroom, doesn't mean that they can utilize the suite of technology to its fullest potential. It's often stated that 90 percent of Excel users use less than 10 percent of the features and capabilities. Have you ever used vLookup commands, or pivot tables?

The same is true for LMSs. In fact, they probably initially utilize less than 10 percent of the overall functionality enabled with student devices and LMS. This is where the SAMR model (substitution, augmentation, modification, and redefinition) was defined, borne of the mode and methods innovated and developed out the need for curriculum that could leverage the features of the new technology.

THE SAMR MODEL

Popularized by Dr. Ruben Puentadura, the model depicts a progression of technology-based evolution of curriculum from SAMR.

Substitution

Substitution is the first rudimentary application of technology application to enhance curriculum. It entails substituting an older technology with a newer one but not really adding significant value to the practicum or curriculum. This concept is commonly referred to as "doing old things, in the old way, with newer stuff."

A sample of technology substitution is commonly seen when a teacher models math exercises under a document camera projected onto a large screen or interactive whiteboard. Although a sophisticated "toolkit" of technology must be present to perform this modeling (projector, interactive display, laptop, document camera), this is only a slight improvement over the overhead projector and transparencies.

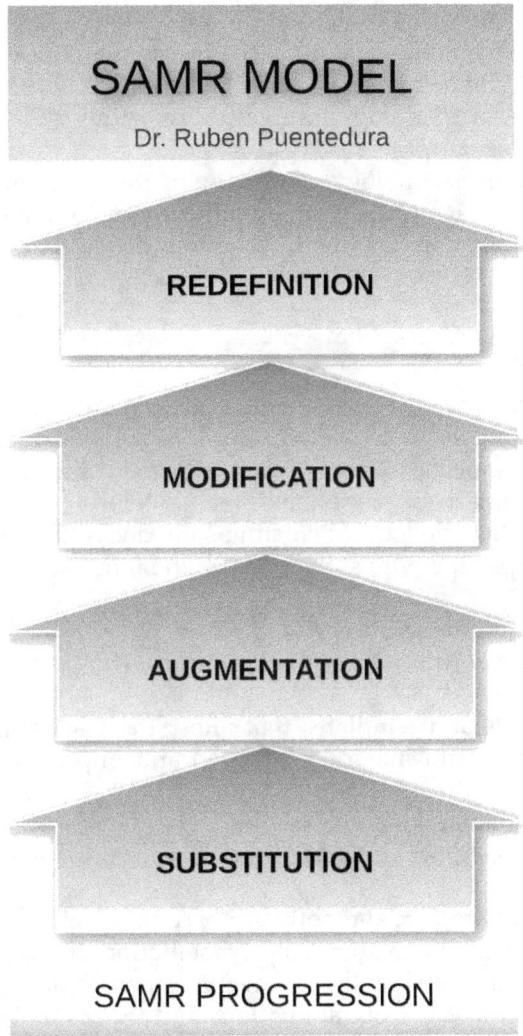

Figure 1.1. SAMR Model.
Source: Dr. Ruben Puentedura

A second and most common example of substitution is using Microsoft PowerPoint to display text-based curriculum slides not significantly different from existing paper-based lesson plans. In this substitution example, it's almost laughable that rudimentary enhancements such as colors, graphics, animations, and videos aren't used to take the curriculum to the next step.

In a higher education example, in my own online master's degree program, one of my philosophy instructors made the most glaring substitution. All prompts were textual, and the posting and delivery process were textual and e-mail based. In essence, the e-mails substituted for pencil, paper, and physically handing the homework into the teacher. Not much technology innovation for either the student or the instructor in this example.

Possibly the only technology advantage of this substitution model is that the homework is not hardcopy. Still, the instructor having to manage homework from as many as one hundred students via e-mail could be very chaotic.

Augmentation

Augmentation is the next level of better integration and enhancement of curriculum utilizing technology. An example of augmentation would be to convert a document-based lesson plan to a PowerPoint presentation, and add some rudimentary graphic enhancements, color, and graphs or tables.

Being a most effective tool for creating slide decks that incorporate the native ability of productivity software with the following features:

- Fonts, outline views, colors
- Import and insertion of graphics: pictures, drawings, photographs, illustrations, etc.
- Drawing tools and templates that allow the teacher to make basic charts, graphs, and integrate captured and imported graphic components.
- The ability to animate graphics.
- The ability to import and add sound, music and videos.

Even though the toolkit and software become a new platform for enhanced communication, creation, and presentation, the curriculum goes largely unchanged. Based on the augmentation example, taking the text-based lesson plan and adding animations and videos make the curriculum slightly more compelling and engaging—but not much. Ultimately, and this will be repeated over and over, it's the teacher who becomes the key to engaging delivery. A boring teacher can make great curriculum boring and vice versa.

These features are so easy to use and feature rich basic text-based curriculum that can be quickly and easily enhanced in a very small amount of time. This is the level of development where the first inkling of templates and standards for graphic "look-and-feel" and navigation will be encountered.

The first teacher to augment existing curriculum using a tool like Microsoft PowerPoint, or Google Slides will begin to implement their own look-and-feel standards—which may immediately conflict with any existing standards that may have been established by others. For instance, one teacher may augment district curriculum using the mascot and color theme of their own school site. Once this curriculum is shared with others outside the school site, the mascot and color theme become nonstandard.

Modification

Modification is the development of new curriculum based on existing curriculum but including new, rich, and diverse media, interactivity, and critical thinking. Using streaming audio and video, interactive exercises, and collaboration platforms may encompass modification of curriculum.

These types of enhancements, modifying existing curriculum to include videos, links, and other practicum utilizing technology systems, such as Internet-based research, video conferences, or virtual field trips, begin to truly enhance the lesson plan and learning experience through new technology capabilities.

But the features and functions that render legacy curriculum as modified would be to integrate technology-based interactions that compel critical thinking skills through context- and scenario-based exercises providing the learner with an experiential-based construct that inserts the learner into an environment seeking to provide a level of realism to the lesson. Instead of describing a swamp, the learner must swim through a swamp—at least in thought, context, and experience.

The other key factor that would raise a curriculum beyond the basic lesson plan outline is collaboration. Whether via e-mail, or LMS, interaction with others in group-work scenarios provide more experiential insight into the study of a lesson.

Redefinition

At the highest level of the SAMR model, curriculum is redesigned and "redefined" to be entirely focused on student critical thinking activities, collaboration and group work, research, and project-based curriculum models. At this level, technology supports many types of learning activities that were not possible without the classroom technology, LMS, video collaboration platforms, vast libraries of content, Internet access, and student devices. In other words, truly "redefined" curriculum could not exist without the basic technology systems and standards.

Using the text-based curriculum example, a redefined curriculum might include video conference lectures, or webinars/podcasts that lead to Internet-based research and analysis/comparison of data (critical thinking), and a final group project that requires each team member to contribute to a collective submission with multiple deliverables including performance-based videos or recordings, 3-D printed or manufactured assemblies, and/or full broadcast video productions such as documentaries or news reports. That raises the question "At what point is this no longer redefinition and simply curriculum development at the highest tier—Tier 4?"

THE LEAPFROG EFFECT

The leapfrog effect takes its name from the schoolyard game of leapfrog where students form a line and the students stoop down while the rearmost student leaps over the others in sequence as the whole chain of students advances forward like a caterpillar. This concept as applied to technology strategy endeavors not to just move forward one step at a time in a gradual progression from status quo to phase 1 and phase 2 but to move from status quo to phase 2 by leapfrogging phase 1 and going directly to phase 2.

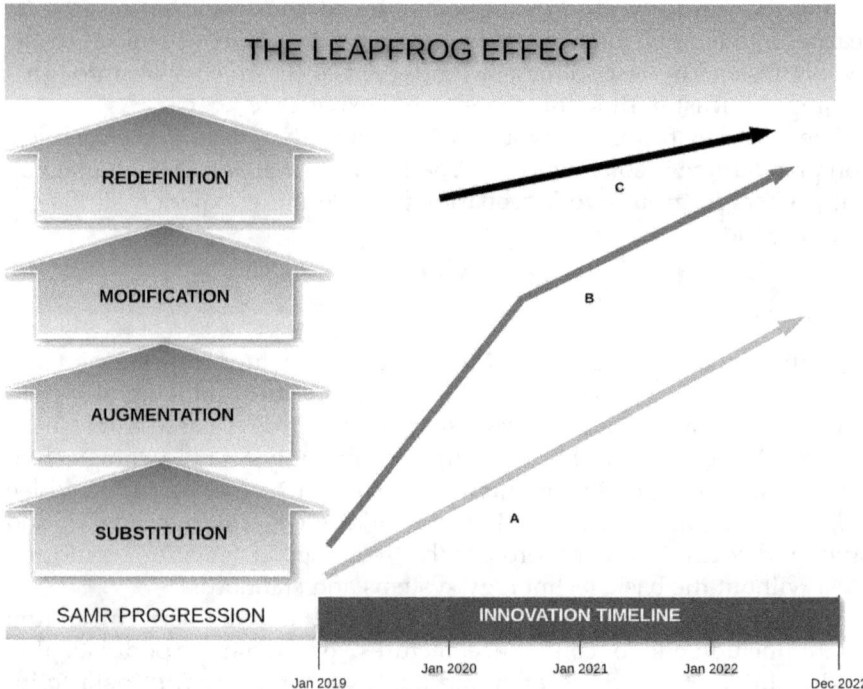

Figure 1.2. The Leapfrog Effect

In effect, if the status quo is currently in a state of ineffectiveness and inefficiency, then addressing and remediating these inefficiencies can be one leap while advancing to strategic innovations at the same time. In Figure 1.2, the A line represents incremental improvement, just achieving the next level. The B line represents a leap beyond the second level for technological advancement to level 3 then eventually to level 4.

The C line represents advancing straight to the highest levels of the model. Like many concepts, this is easy to describe, but how do we make it a reality? That is the focus of this book.

DISRUPTION

The concept of disruption is well documented both for business as well as in education. The book *Disrupting Class* by Clayton Christensen (2017) has been widely read in education communities. Fundamentally, the concept is akin to the leapfrog effect but to a more significant impact.

Instead of incremental and sequential improvements and innovations, disruption breaks the progression and redefines a new starting point well beyond the classic incremental progression. By seeking to disrupt the typical path of improvement and innovation, the strategy seeks to move beyond the traditional metrics and milestones and set a broader set of goals and a faster pace.

SAMR DISRUPTION

The SAMR disruption model overlays the concept of disruption to the SAMR model. Instead of a school district focusing on moving up the model in succession, the curriculum development and PD should focus on leap-frogging the augmentation and modification stages and moving directly to redefinition.

Obviously, this concept and vision requires strategic planning, technology infrastructure, and investment and implementation planning in concert with PD. We'll take up this discussion later in the T4c section of this book, but before that, one must understand what the steps of the progression are.

In order to leap over these steps, it doesn't mean they can be ignored—quite the opposite, in fact. It means these levels and the reality of current infrastructure, curriculum, and teaching staff must assimilate all these advancements in order to exist at the top of the model—totally redefined curriculum.

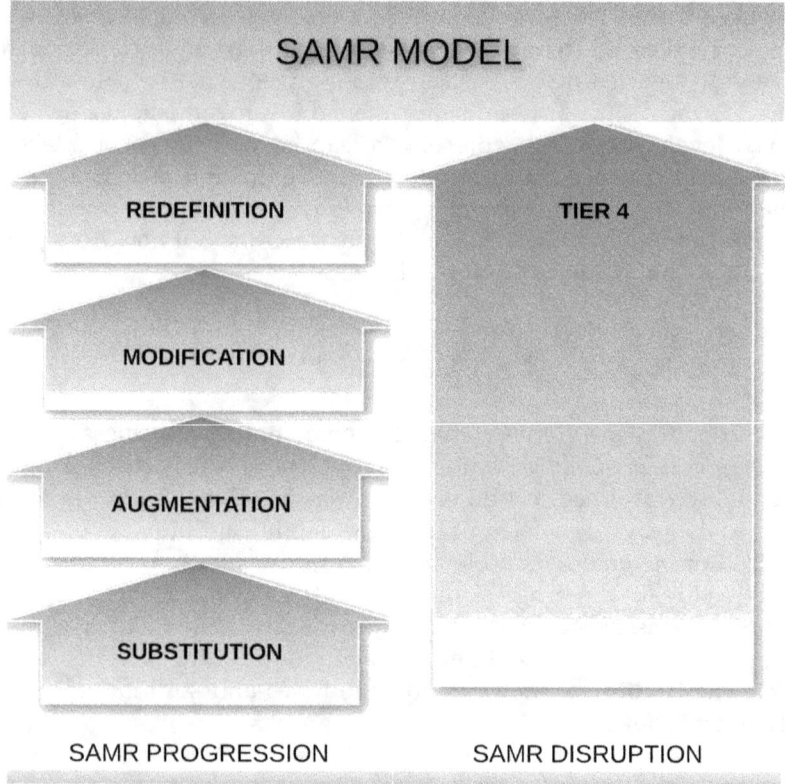

Figure 1.3. Jump Straight to Tier 4

The next section takes a detailed look at what that progression would look like if a school or district took these steps one at a time in a logical progression, one step building on all the previous. Examining your school from this perspective gives you the ability to assess whether this type of advancement can be attained because ultimately, if all the infrastructure and curriculum is available, execution is entirely dependent on staff. To examine this evolution capacity within your organization, consider the following instructional and technological innovation strategy.

CHAPTER 1—ACTION ITEMS

Since this book is not just a concept book—it's about implementation—it will provide you with all the guidance necessary to disrupt your school's status quo. At the end of each chapter of this book are action items. As spelled out in our MAPIT® Project Management books, this book will manage your district through this disruption.

The action items assume you are one of the chosen few who have the vision, standing, and ambition to lead your school or district straight to implementation of the promise of education technology.

1. *Identify your school's VISION for education technology*
   Starting with your district's LCAP and board goals and objectives, see if these plans provide enough guidance and direction to base an innovative instructional initiative.
2. *Assess your organization for instructional innovation*
   Start to put the word out in your district that you're looking for teachers doing innovative things with technology. How are teachers doing more innovative things with the district's current curriculum? See who in the instructional services department might be the top innovator.
3. *Assess your organization for tech bias*
   Assess if your education technology staff or IT department is imposing a tech bias on instruction. Are the technology leaders providing platforms and standards that teachers can leverage in their classrooms?
4. *Assess your school's posture for SAMR and SAMR disruption*
   Make an effort to see if your district instructional staff and teachers are aware of the SAMR model. If so, what is being done to inspire innovative strategies that move your district's teachers and platforms up the model.

Chapter 2

Instructional and Technological Innovation Strategy

The Innovation Strategy chart (Figure 2.1) details an example of an improvement strategy for both the instructional technology and information technology services departments. The progression (starting from the bottom) shows factors of inefficiency and ineffectiveness that may be symptoms of dysfunction or lack of structure or process below the *line of discontent*, and progressively complex initiatives and integrations moving up from the line.

This is not to state that your district's organizations are at or below the line of discontent, only to demonstrate how an improvement and innovation strategy might deliver more complex and innovative instructional and operational support systems. But first the items below the line of discontent must be mitigated and overcome. Some organizations languish here for eternity.

The higher levels of this strategy focus on more leveraged and complex integrations, customizations, and instructional trends. Many of these systems and technologies may address high-level district objectives like pathways, parent, and community engagement, and the improvement of staff through professional development (PD) and data analytics.

Once again, infrastructure must be in place, relevant data must be collected, warehoused, and then analyzed and reported. Data analytics is the integration of multiple data sources and developing reports based on these new data stores. Once again, PD within both the instructional and technology sides of the organization become the key in moving up from the basics.

Staff members don't know what they don't know, so someone must offer a vision and objectives, then provide them with training resources and opportunities. Even if the decision is to outsource integrating and development work, the internal resources for defining and managing the resources still must have the base-level understanding and capability to manage these systems over time.

Only then can decision support systems, high-level curriculum, web portals, and communities of learners proliferate.

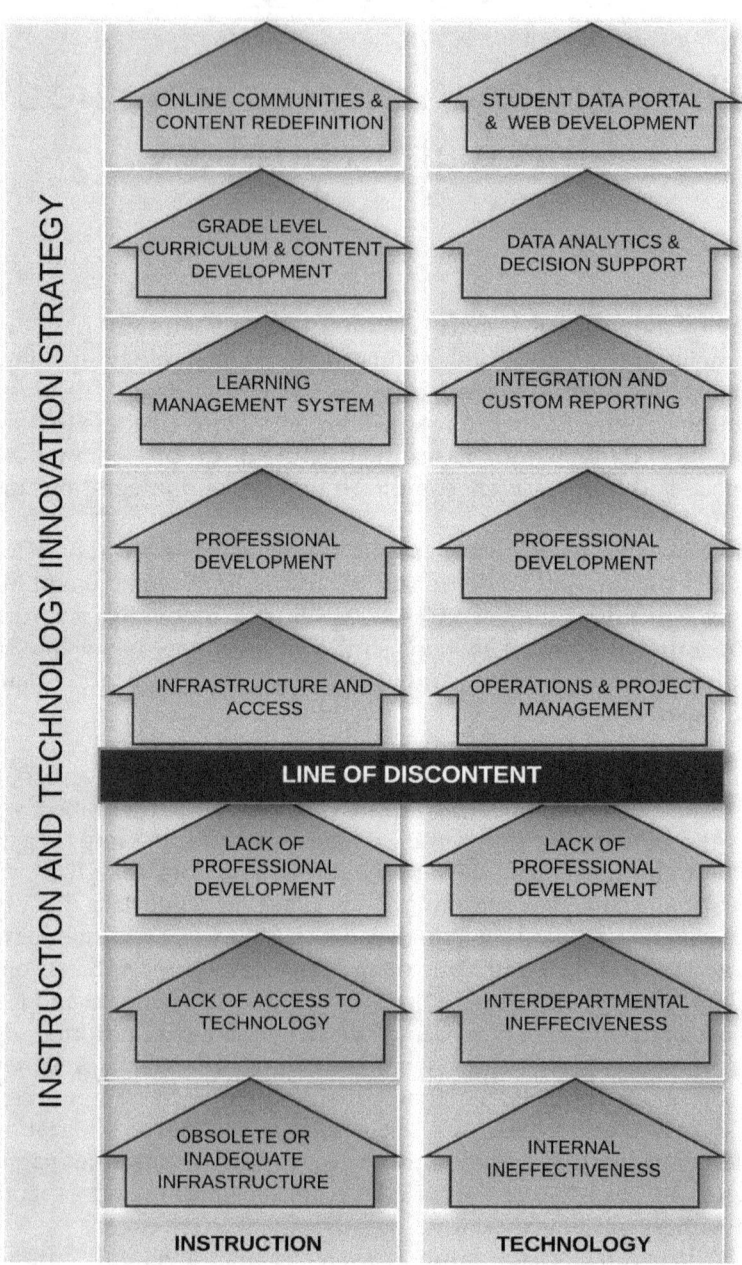

Figure 2.1. Instruction and Technology Innovation Strategy

Instructional and Technological Innovation Strategy

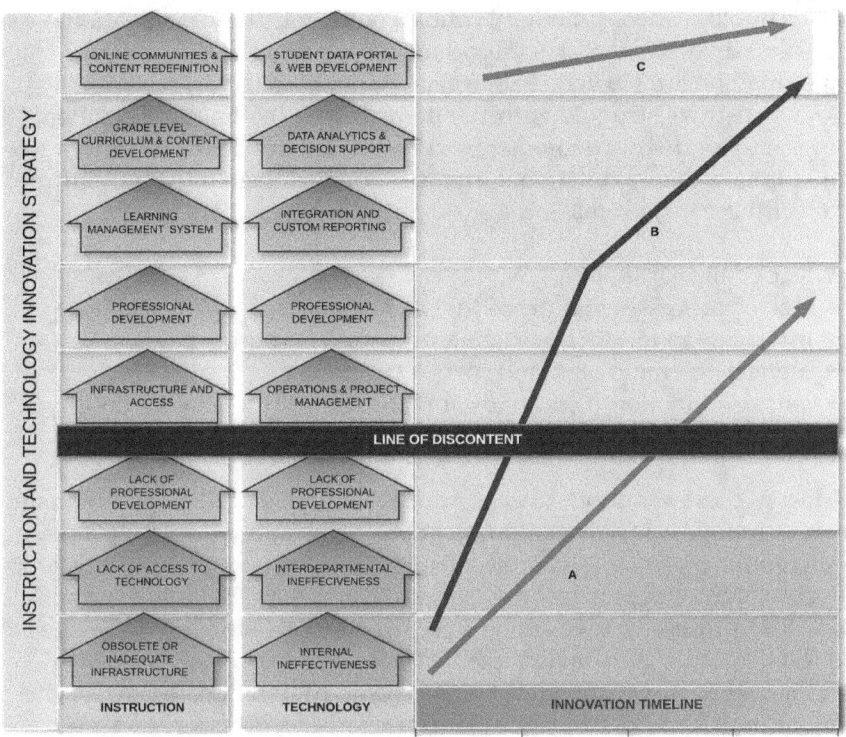

Figure 2.2. Disrupting the SAMR Model

On the instruction side—use of LMS (learning management system), content development, and content redefinition (SAMR; substitution, augmentation, modification, and redefinition) are on the top. On the technical side—integration of data systems and reporting, analytics and decision support, and student access to performance and outreach services top the list.

Figure 2.2 overlays the disruption path on top of the Instruction and Technology Innovation Strategy chart. If an organization suffers from the symptoms below the line of discontent, an aggressive instruction and technology improvement strategy must be outlined to address each area before an organization can even consider the innovation strategies above the line of discontent.

BELOW THE LINE OF DISCONTENT

The instruction and technology innovation strategy chart details some of the challenges of dysfunction within a school or district's instructional and technology departments. Without revisiting the organizational aspects already discussed, it is important to note that the fundamental challenges may be infrastructure or organizationally related.

Many districts struggle with the items below the line of discontent. If your school or district demonstrates these attributes below the line, a fundamental and likely functional organizational change must be instituted to affect these symptoms and issues. These can be factors of

- leadership, or lack of,
- lack of processes and procedures,
- discipline in following existing processes and procedures,
- ineffective employees, and/or
- any combination of individual or groups of dissension, dissatisfaction or outright sabotage.

Most of these symptoms can be addressed with simple project management techniques such as communications plans and workflow processes. Implementing processes can often be the key to solving workflow problems by taking the personalities out of the equation. By following simple workflow processes, there is no need to ask for favors or make special requests. In fact, personality conflicts can be completely mitigated by eliminating personal interaction and using automation to bypass these manual processes.

For instance, if a process is currently like this:

When the educational services assistant superintendent has a reporting requirement, he goes to the analyst in the information technology (IT) department and describes what he wants.

- This is ineffective because the assistant superintendent doesn't know how to specify the reporting requirements so the analyst must make broad assumptions.
- Sometimes because this process is uncomfortable, the analyst just says it can't be done.

It could be mitigated by automation by doing this:

- When the education services assistant superintendent has a reporting requirement, he must fill out a form request online and provide the report specification from the agency requesting the report.
- This opens a service ticket that is then assigned to the IT director to assign to an analyst and tracked.
- Once the project is complete the assistant superintendent is provided the report.

Project requirements are simply planned out in advance and assigned to responsible resources. All stakeholders become aware of responsibilities and tasks in the critical path. When tasks and responsibilities are clearly defined and assigned, most stakeholders will have very little patience for missing pleasantries, hurt feelings, and hidden agendas.

Some of the items below the line may be factors of budget and resources, but these are inherently rooted in lack of strategic planning. In that case, read *Fail to Plan, Plan to Fail* (Vidal 2017), which is specifically about "How to Create Your School's Education Technology Strategic Plan."

That's not to say that a technology strategic plan can positively affect personnel or budgetary challenges, but a technology strategic plan should endeavor to improve academic impact using technology. The plan should also identify possible funding and resources to implement changes. Without this plan the organizational leadership has nothing to demonstrate their commitment or even recognition that these challenges exist.

Once a district has overcome the fundamental challenges below the line of discontent, they can then focus on the district's move up the model for technology adoption and innovation.

Starting on the side of instruction, obsolete or inadequate infrastructure is possibly the largest obstacle to any type of high-level curriculum development and adoption. Without a base-level of technology enabling systems in place and without basic staff proficiency, there can be no development or widespread implementation of technology-based curriculum.

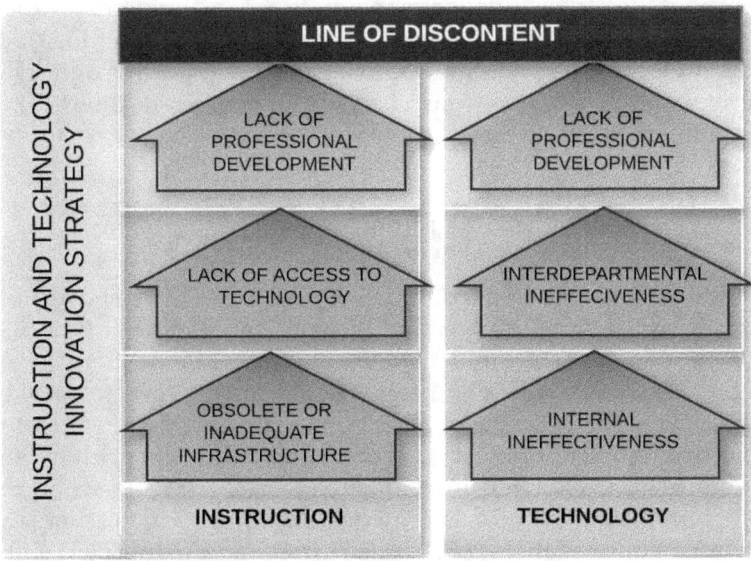

Figure 2.3. Below the Line of Discontent

Forget cognitive versus critical thinking models. Without the technology infrastructure, which includes LANs, WANs, Internet, firewalls, classroom technology, and devices, there will be no movement up the SAMR spectrum.

Lack of access to technology for the user base (student laptops or Chromebooks, home computer/Internet access, and smartphones) presents the same issues as lack of infrastructure. Every school must deal with equity and access in order to begin the ascent up the innovation strategy.

Finally, PD provides the grease to the seized wheel. It cannot be expected that teachers already know how to take their legacy curriculum and begin the progression up the SAMR model without guidance, coaching, and developmental support.

On the technology side of the strategy, the functionality of IT department operations becomes the key. Is the IT department utilizing a call-tracking (problem management) and/or help desk system? These processes are the key to departmental effectiveness, which in turn leads to district and instructional effectiveness. Only the smallest organizations can stay organized and on task without these support applications.

If projects and initiatives seem to come to a halt passing from edict through to implementation, then intra- and interdepartmental workflows are flawed or nonexistent. Once again, these types of organizational dysfunction can be addressed and remediated with the implementation of project management procedures, controls, and automation.

Interdepartmental effectiveness occurs when workflows pass cleanly and seamlessly between departments without incurring delays, lapses in task responsibility or accountability, and/or delays in timing or priority. Stakeholders are up to date because of status reporting and scheduling. Project resources are on task because of communications planning in engagement.

MOVING ABOVE THE LINE OF DISCONTENT

Considering the Technology Innovation Strategies chart above the line, the reader will notice a progression of more and more complex integrations, reporting, and custom development offerings.

On the instruction side, the district would offer a comprehensive curriculum development platform that allows rapid development and rapid deployment of standards-based curriculum. The curriculum should incorporate full Common Core State Standards (CCSS), focus on critical thinking, problem solving, and provide tools for extensive asynchronous and synchronous collaboration. These curriculum modules would be accessed online via LMS or online communities.

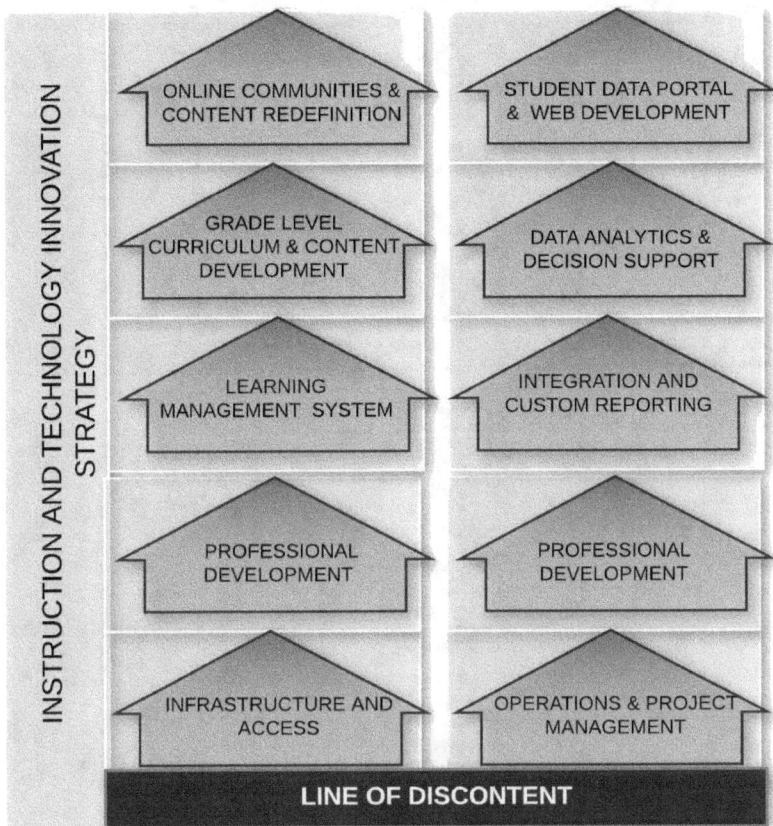

Figure 2.4. Above the Line of Discontent

On the technology side, the integration and development of customized reports (for compliance and internal reporting), then leads to data analytics to inform staff and administration. From there, the next step leads up to all these data types and reports, available in detail and dashboards, in a secure and private matter to the district and community at large via a web portal—the same web portal that delivers the instructional content.

Let's look at the progression from each side individually.

Instructional Innovation Strategy

Moving up the instructional side of the model, we'll see how the need for infrastructure—a lowest common denominator—must be standardized and ubiquitous to begin a district-wide impact.

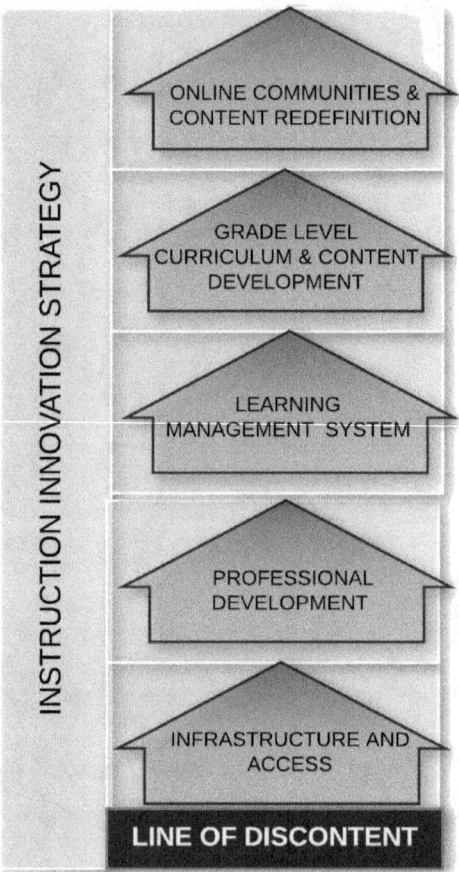

Figure 2.5.   Instructional Innovation Strategy

INFRASTRUCTURE AND ACCESS

Infrastructure without access diminishes the impact of any technology initiative to those lacking the direct access. Installing a wireless infrastructure and then only purchasing mobile devices for grade levels will limit the overall impact and not expand organically. Those that matriculate out of the "beneficiary group" will quickly lose the skills developed while immersed in the technology.

This reality is true for both the students as well as the teachers. If only secondary teachers will get new technology systems, then what of the nonbeneficiaries? Will they not be able to participate in the curricular advances of the beneficiaries? What if some schools are selected while others must wait? How will the rollout be prioritized?

All these questions shed no light on the solution except for *planning* and money. Initiatives and implementations that spend the money on technologies but don't plan effectively in relation to balanced infrastructure and access will have some valid frustrations to deal with. The more logical and sensical and well communicated the strategy, the better opportunity for the plan to be accepted.

Professional Development

PD is the next stage of the progression. First the ability and skill sets of the teachers to understand and utilize the standard classroom technology requires proficiency in the platform operating system, access to the network and Internet, and familiarity with a productivity suite, whether it be MS Office or Google Apps for Education.

Most training and educational courses are delivered over a time frame with an objective and lesson plan. Unfortunately, staff PD is often slammed into hours of in-service training, funneled alongside learning to use the student information system, grading, and now the LMS platform. To that add additional training, coaching, and/or mentoring for robotics, science lab, coding, makerspaces, and video production—good luck!

PD can also be led organically, first by defining and developing a course of research and practice. Individuals can pursue self-paced learning, fully immersed in the LMS and development platform.

Learning Management System

The LMS becomes the lifeblood of the curriculum delivery. Like it or not, the more the teaching staff learns and assimilates the usage of the LMS features and functions, the more immersed the students become in the learning context. Just as the importance of the doors, windows, classrooms, lighting, and plumbing of a school campus becomes irrelevant, the student becomes unaware but explicitly dependent on the LMS.

Think of how online learning has evolved to the point where higher education can be done online and/or remotely without a perceivable lack of functional negative impact. There is literally nothing that renders online learning less capable than hybrid or traditional campus-based learning. Take away catching viruses and parking and the online experience becomes preferable, especially for working adults. With most colleges and universities offering programs entirely online, there's really no reason to visit the bricks-and-mortar campus.

The amount of instructor and peer interaction is not diminished virtually by any means. In fact, the asynchronous aspect of message boards and remote synchronous meetings make interpersonal communication and group work fully functional. The only time peers meet face-to-face would be on graduation day. How far this functionality can be pushed down in K–12 education is yet to be tested.

Campus-based school for primary/elementary education will always be the basis as the social interaction in the physical classroom context must be experienced directly. Adults can take on the online experience as a substitute for the physical presence and social interaction already learned in the physical school, but early learners will have no context for social interaction in a virtual classroom scenario.

The point of this discussion is not that some teachers must learn to use the LMS, then others might as well. The objective is that when all teachers are effectively using all the features, then all the students will draw the maximum benefit of the platform, which is to say that all students will become familiar with multimedia and multimodal learning, electronic submission and assessment of work, messaging and collaboration, group work and leadership roles, performance delivery, and advance work products like publications or broadcast productions.

A highly leveraged effect occurs when all teachers and all students use the LMS to full function. The LMS itself becomes a virtual version of the school/campus in the cloud, with specific advantages over the bricks-and-mortar campus:

- Synchronous becomes asynchronous—Anything that happens on the LMS is archived for perpetuity. Even synchronous video chats can be recorded and viewed after the fact. The concept of missing a classroom lecture completely vanishes.
- Enforced scheduling—In the bricks-and-mortar campus, students must arrive physically on campus. If the hours of time wasted parking and walking are estimated in the overall time for school activity, the number would blow your mind. Less than half the time spent in classes and getting to and from campus and to classrooms is educational. In the virtual classroom all you do is wait for class to start and the connection is on the computer (if it's a synchronous class), students can never be late because of parking or traffic.
- Personal appearance becomes a nonfactor—Save the discussion about appearances and speech. Let it be understood, however, that any positive or negative effects a person's appearance, speech, and/or interpersonal skills might impact their educational experience on campus and in face-to-face situations can be completely mitigated in the virtual classroom.
- Multiple interactions—In the classroom environment, if everyone speaks at the same time, the classroom turns into chaos, discus-

sions are lost, and confusion reigns. In the interactive message boards, infinite conversations can go on simultaneously. Individual students can converse with others or in groups. The teacher(s) can monitor, manage, and assess interactions, both in quantity, through statistics and reports, and in quality by reviewing the message content and interactions.
- Iterative submissions—In the legacy homework scenario, the teacher gives an assignment, the student takes it home and completes it, then turns it in the next day. The assignment is graded, maybe notes are written, the grade recorded, and the homework returned to the student. In the LMS scenario, the teacher posts homework in the class homework folder along with due dates and instructions and materials. The student completes the work online at their convenience and submits. The teacher can review and assess the work and even return it to the student for additional revision. This revision opportunity can go on infinitely at the teacher's discretion and capacity, to allow the teacher to ensure that each student is afforded maximum teacher interactions.
- Time stamp and authenticity—The LMS has built-in controls such as time stamps and due dates. There's no, "my dog ate my homework" or "I had a flat tire" excuses on the LMS. If something is due by midnight, it will not be accepted one second after midnight—no excuses. Plagiarism review systems are also integrated to check for original work. This is a capability entirely owned by the online world. There was no plagiarism review system even as far as twenty-five years ago.

Grade Level Curriculum and Content Development

The whole point of this book is this section of the instructional innovation strategy. The meat of this book details how to develop the Tier 4 curriculum (T4c) using a process called 6C development. The innocuous names will make perfect sense when those chapters are discussed, but this fourth stage to the innovation strategy is reliant and built upon the LMS and infrastructure. Any discussion of curriculum development must also address the Ws: Who, What, When, Where, and Why?

Development of curriculum using technology is a complicated subject from its core. Unless there is already a designated team in the instructional services department, most districts would be hard-pressed to develop a plan for a district-standardized technology-based curriculum development team. It's easy to imagine the headcount—knowing there's librarians and media techs who could do some of these tasks, but they typically aren't the subject matter experts (SMEs).

In fact, SMEs are a whole discussion by itself. Are there SMEs out at the sites? Of course. Are the district instructional resources SMEs? Maybe on some subjects. Are the SMEs also the development resources? It is not likely that all of them have the same skill levels.

Think about the diversity of skills and backgrounds behind developing a history, math, or science curriculum, leveraging technology *and* developing lesson plans and content according to a set of district standards for technology-based curriculum. There are also people in the IT department who can do these things, but they're not educators, and they have no idea about lesson planning, state standards, and classroom management.

Unfortunately, even though this book discusses how to develop curriculum for the technology-enabled school, it doesn't answer all these questions about resources and their employ. It does however provide a plan to implement T4c development organically, at the classroom and site level. District resources will still be necessary to facilitate the standardization, centralization, and warehousing of the content, but this book will provide the roadmap for the core development process. So, keep reading.

ONLINE COMMUNITIES

The most advanced form of technology innovation through the current era is online communities, also known as communities of learning. Once curriculum in developed in a T4c context, it would be able to be shared in a portal or warehouse, where ultimately it can be part of an overall curriculum package which can be completed online, assessed and tracked for certification in a program of study.

Under this construct, students would be able to work forward and complete curriculum and a course of study at their own pace and without sacrificing substantiated learning through assessment and standardized testing, but also allowing advanced and high-achieving students to complete multiple courses of study in the standard K–12 school year. Imagine completing high school with multiple college advanced placement (AP) courses in multiple disciplines.

Technology Innovation Strategy

Many school IT departments languish below the line of discontent, mired in internal ineffectiveness, interdepartmental ineffectiveness, and lack of PD. Software and systems are implemented to track and improve these processes, but these processes and systems don't run themselves, people do. It is also recognized that processes and systems need to change over time. The process for ordering a new typewriter is different from ordering a new computer.

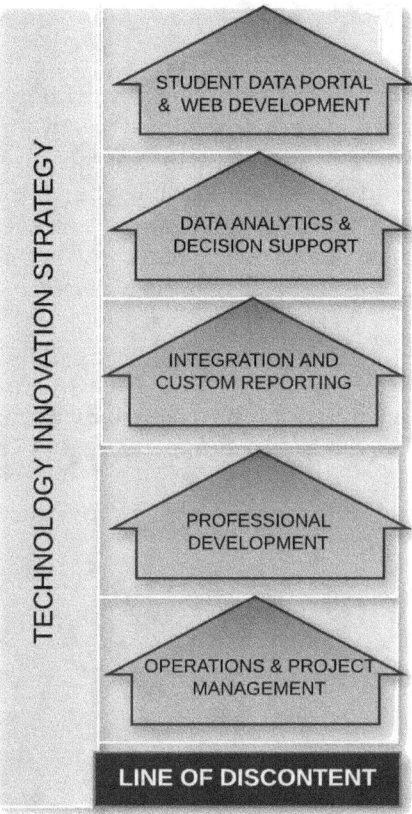

Figure 2.6. Technology Innovation Strategy

Similarly, the process for getting the typewriter fixed is rudimentary to getting a computer, network, or the Internet fixed. Another example is the help desk and call-tracking system itself. Just because the process was defined by "such and such" person ten years ago doesn't mean that the systems and priorities haven't changed. The legacy architectures and systems must be strategically planned for improvement over time just like the lifecycle of technology equipment.

This process is well documented in the author's previous book, *Project Management in the Ed Tech Era: How to Successfully Plan and Manage Your School's Next Innovation*, where the process of analyzing, planning, and operationalizing IT projects to solve both intra- and interdepartmental workflow is discussed in gory detail. So, once the people plan and implement the operational processes and systems, a school IT department can move above the line of discontent and begin moving up the technology innovation path.

OPERATIONS AND PROJECT MANAGEMENT

Upon achieving operational effectiveness in the IT department, both intradepartmental and interdepartmental workflows can be improved and enhanced with the continuous improvement lifecycle. The lifecycle defines the steps IT organizations use to first measure, and then improve, based on metrics, trend analysis, knowledge base development, and process improvement.

Starting at the top, goals and objectives for the organization are defined. Each functional work group and team can perform a similar subtasked process improvement cycle as well. From these goals, the department's rules, roles, and tools are analyzed and assessed for their effectiveness in their current application and purpose. An action plan is developed for each identified opportunity for improvement by documenting the fault or deficiency, performing a root cause analysis, and developing a mitigation or remediation plan.

Let's look at an example of a process improvement in a typical IT department.

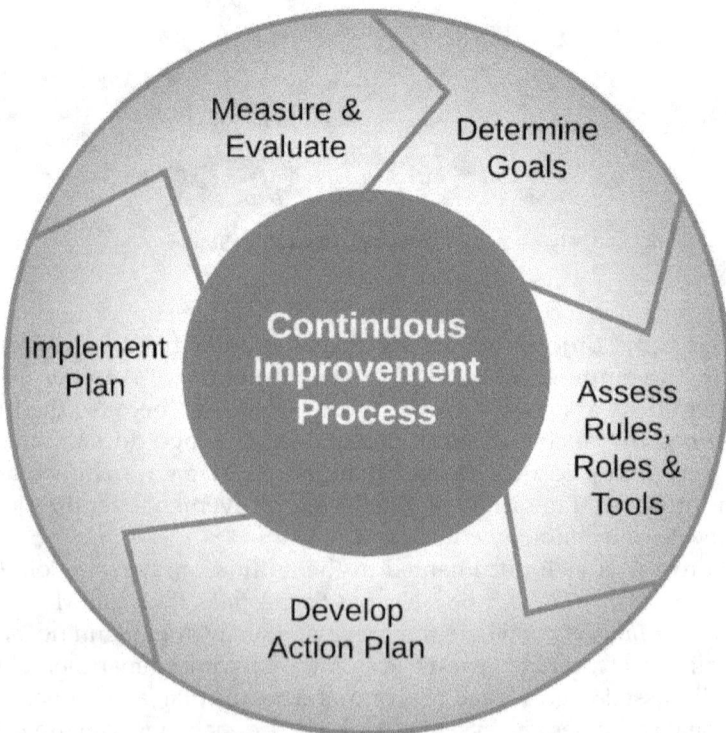

Figure 2.7.   Continuous Improvement Process

Table 2.1. Problem Categories

Problem Categories	Hardware	Software	Network
Subcategories	Computer	Operating System	Switch
	Printer	Office	Router
	Laptop	Database	Firewall
	Thin Client	Financials	Phone

An IT department has started collecting and tracking problem distribution data in their help desk tracking system by increasing the granularity of their problem categories, where in the past they only had hardware issues, software issues, network issues, and Internet issues. They added another layer of categorization.

Hardware—Computer, Printer, Network Switch, etc.
Software—Operating System, Productivity, Custom, App
Network—Wireless, Firewall, Internet

Once these additional subcategories were being tracked, they could produce a problem distribution report that showed the most common problems each month. From this information, they could develop a response or training plan to address and mitigate problems of the previous month.

Project management communications techniques can make a difference in intra- and interdepartmental correspondence. By implementing a request for communications workflow, a document and approval process reinforces the legacy "ask and you may receive" process.

By standardizing the request format and requirements, the requestor and requestee are given the same information in a previously accepted format. Within this process, a service level of response and delivery time can be estimated and enforced if needed. By using e-mail, or another time-stamped communication platform, the request is formally submitted and memorialized.

The personal idiosyncrasies of individuals are detached from the process. Time stamps are there to enforce service levels and time commitments. Names of requestors, requestees, and approvers are copied on the e-mails to reinforce communication to stakeholders and approvers and enforce accountability.

Professional Development

PD for IT departmental staff is completely different from the instructional side of the district. Where teacher PD impacts the areas of computer, web, and productivity application proficiency, curriculum planning, development, and implementation, IT staff want to be trained on routing, switching, Wi-Fi, security, and server and device management.

IT staff should be pursuing a track for certification training in Windows, VMWare, cybersecurity, and network management. Project and administrative staff might pursue PMI training and or application-based training. The state or county office of education(s) typically provide training for relevant systems and services offered by the agency/departments. IT PD is both practical in terms of expanded resource capability as well as personal in terms of individual staff members' self-improvement and overall morale boosting.

Integration and Custom Reporting

The next step up the technology innovation ladder is the integration of systems and customization of reporting capabilities. This requires an application development capability/resource in the district, or an outsourced entity might be more cost effective.

These resources are often in various departments and groups in the legacy organization and with varying degrees of expertise. Sometimes there are analysts that can work on MS Access but cannot write SQL scripts, or the Crystal Reports analyst can't import/export to the county/state API.

Part of the challenge is finding and engaging the resources that can integrate the platforms. Often these limited resources are entirely tapped out on other projects and cannot be scheduled for reporting projects, but the ability to customize business platforms, import/export, and integrate is the most difficult. Start by developing formal report requests through the formal change control processes and escalate until the necessary resources are identified.

The district has to find and foster integration and customization resources so that they aren't held hostage by vendors and unreliable freelancers. These skill sets must be developed in-house if the district truly seeks to continue to integrate and leverage their data and reporting capabilities.

True programmers/analysts must be recruited and employed with the appropriate skill set for application development and database administration. Promoting classroom teachers and TOSAs (teachers on special assignment) into technical development scopes will not advance the department as quickly as engaging the correct skill sets from the beginning of the initiative.

Once the ability to integrate and customize a school's business, student information, and reporting systems is accomplished, a whole new opportunity for technology innovation presents itself at the next level.

Student Data Portal and Web Development

Web portal development can be facilitated in many ways. This may be determined by investment made into the current web portal platform, or a full development crew might use a more low-level development environment that provides more customization.

Once the district can address the immediate reporting challenges through the identification and engagement of (internal or external) resources, the next stage will be to achieve the highest level of data customization and delivery via a web-based portal.

Students and their parents should have secure portal access to all attendance, assessment, and testing data that is made available by the district to the state. They should also have secure access to personal, enrollment, and emergency data that should be accessed securely online.

A student data portal should provide students and parents access to their most relevant information, as well as provide information on bus routes and schedules, school lunch and cafeteria programs, and individualized education programs (IEPs), in addition to California Assessment of Student Performance and Progress (CAASPP) and Smarter Balanced Assessment Consortium (SBAC) data.

The student data portal should provide access to the LMS, lesson plans, curriculum modules, assessments, and communities of learning (message and chat boards, video conferencing, and other hosting of synchronous and asynchronous communications, collaboration, and group work). Pathways and school-to-work programs should also be accessible via the portal.

ED TECH STATUS QUO AND INNOVATION

After understanding the instructional technology innovation strategy, the reader can see that by taking baby steps up the ladder, they are building the following:

1. Infrastructure—making technology systems ubiquitous
2. Skills and Capabilities—understanding and leveraging the LMS
3. Content Development—the ability to take existing content/curriculum and develop customized, multimedia/multimodal curriculum that leverages the LMS and infrastructure
4. Web Community of Learning—providing a portal to access, manage, and inform students, parents, and their community

If your school or district hasn't taken step 1, you will never get to step 4.

IT STATUS QUO

Similarly, within the IT department, status quo means standing still or treading water. IT operations, network operations, cybersecurity, and IT support *must* be on an improvement cycle. IT systems must get faster, more robust, and fully integrated, otherwise the organization will be forced to make painful steps forward using manual processes. The promise of automation and value-add only comes from technology innovation.

This also implies a request/fulfillment process between business departments and the IT applications development department. Any business department should be able to work with IT to define new integrations/reporting needs, specify them formally, commit resources and time frames, and develop these new capabilities.

What? Your IT department doesn't do this? It also raises the question of how the applications and reporting resources are getting completed and how resources are tracking their work requests. If they're not made formally with a report output specification, then how are these development projects being tracked and monitored? How is their delivery monitored and validated?

CHALLENGING PAST PRACTICES AND LEGACY PROCEDURES

The most important aspect of innovation is not to be beholden to past practices and legacy procedures. How often has someone questioned a process or form in your organization and asked, "Why do we do it this way?" only to be met with, "That's the way I was taught." Or "That's the way so-and-so did it." Or the most notorious, "We've tried to change it but, so-and-so won't let us."

Any IT head that isn't in the process of automating manual legacy processes is either an enabler or a victim. They are not an innovator. All IT heads must understand the need and the process to automate. Any hardcopy form must be eliminated—now! Call us directly if you need help! There is no current-day reason for any person in your school district to fill out a manual hardcopy form. Sorry to tell you. If you get one of these answers, you're going to have to object and offer to automate it. Remember all the infrastructure, skills, and capabilities just built in the previous sections. If you can't automate, then you need to understand why—be the disrupter.

These types of interactions are anti-innovation. These legacies must be challenged all the way to the highest level, even if you have to say, "With all due respect. . . ." Doing things the old way is rarely the best way. However, it must be reliable, otherwise it would have been changed long ago. So, the questioner must be aware that any new process or procedure must ensure the same level of reliability. Sometimes this is where automation is suspect, because the legacy stakeholders will say, "That won't work because. . . ." Then, if for some reason, the automation failed, you may never regain that political capital. Be the innovator on the "leading edge," not on the "bleeding edge."

In the IT world, it is understood that automation of manual processes is the *only* way to ensure data integrity. For production systems that impact revenue and profits, data integrity is everything. School operations are paid for from funding based on average daily attendance (ADA), which is their primary revenue source. So, student information, attendance, and tardiness are the revenue metrics, and they are just as important as sales in a corporation.

In the curriculum world, these issues are less stringent but just as important to protect privacy and security. In curriculum (except for mathematics) a little leeway here and there is an acceptable risk assuming state and district standards are adhered to.

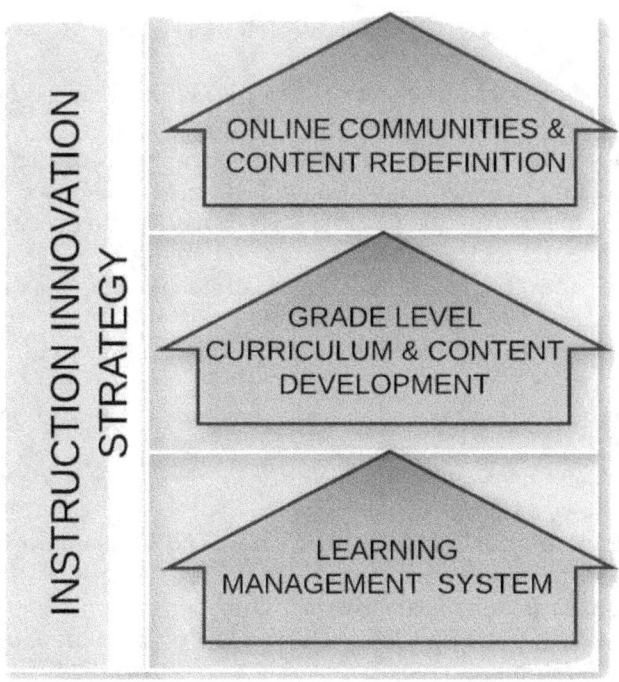

Figure 2.8. Instructional Innovation Strategy—Top Levels

It's a good practice to ask the question, *How can this process be improved?* And, *How can this process be automated?* anytime an inefficient or manual process is encountered. It is never a good business practice to use spreadsheets in a business production process because nothing is more uncontrolled than a bunch of users generating reports with Excel. Who's checking if their source data is valid and up to date? How are the calculations checked for errors and validated? There's basically no assurance of data integrity when end users can copy and paste formulas into spreadsheets and generate tables and graphs.

Challenging the past procedures and legacy processes is an important aspect of strategic planning as well as tactical planning. And there's always more to it than just moving forward and doing it. There's stakeholders and existing systems, third parties, and county and state agencies. You can't just tell the California Department of Education that they're doing things the old-fashioned way.

For this book, we're looking to help schools and districts define a method to create and implement T4c at the largest scale—district wide. So now take the next step—a deep dive into the top level of instructional technology innovation, the top of the SAMR model, Tier 4 curriculum—T4c.

CHAPTER 2—ACTION ITEMS

1. *Assess your instructional and IT departments for symptoms below the line of discontent*

    Does your district and schools have the necessary technology infrastructure to foster innovation of technology enhanced curriculum?

    Does the instructional services team have all the necessary equipment, cloud services, and access to technology?

    Does the IT department demonstrate internal departmental effectiveness?

    Are they responsive to the district departments, with all information reporting requests?

    Do the instruction and IT teams have exposure and opportunities for PD?

2. *Assess your instructional and IT innovation strategy relative to the Innovation Strategy Model*

    Compare your district's instruction and IT teams relative to the innovation strategy.

3. *Assess your improvement strategy*

    How will your district get to the top of the Innovation Strategy Model? You must develop a plan.

CHAPTER 3

Key Technology Systems/Features

In the current state of the educational technology landscape, any individual school or district could have any variety of technology standards—or none at all. This book will detail how to develop curriculum at the most advanced models of instructional technology incorporating all matters of technology capabilities from synchronous/asynchronous, media rich, collaborative, and virtual models.

In order to develop content standards and implement them at a district level, minimum standard technologies (technical capabilities) must exist within each classroom and the site. Capabilities of hardware, software, and infrastructure are required, as well as basic skills both at the teacher and student levels. Following are key technology systems and how they must be implemented and ubiquitous within the school in order to support the Tier 4 Curriculum (T4c) concept.

LEARNING MANAGEMENT SYSTEMS

Learning management systems (LMSs) provide the core of online learning just as a physical campus forms the basic infrastructure of a traditional school. The buildings have openings and stairs to access the various classrooms and shared facilities. There are basic components in each classroom: desks, chairs, lectern, and whiteboard (chalkboard).

There are infrastructure and facilities to accommodate the specific needs of the tenants: restrooms, playgrounds, multipurpose rooms, teacher lounges, and media centers. Electricity, air-conditioning, and fire alarms provide for safety and environmental controls.

LMSs must provide similar technology capabilities for each student and teacher as well as the physical classrooms they are assigned. It should accommodate a variety of user types such as student, teacher, and administrator that provide and restrict functionality according to

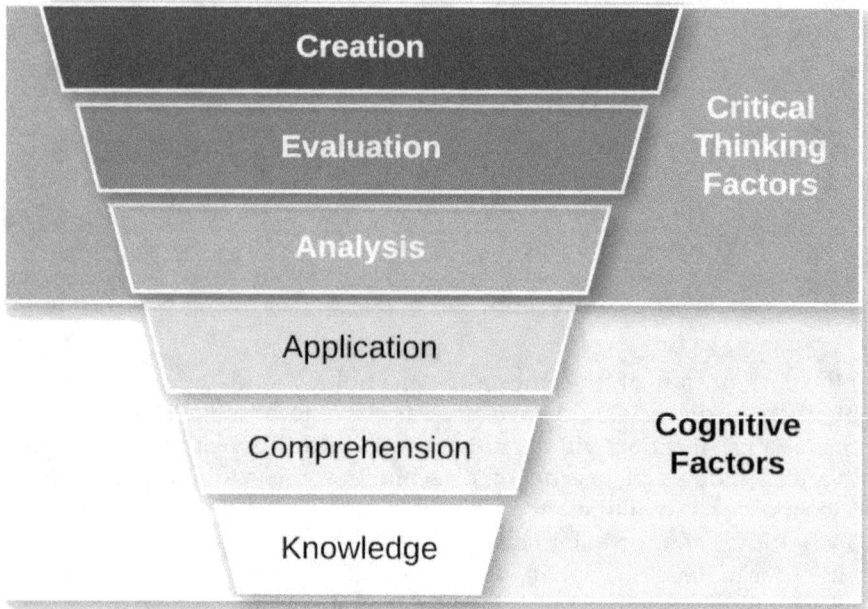

Figure 3.1. Bloom's Taxonomy

the user type. Just as the teacher has keys to their classroom and the custodian has keys to all the classrooms, the LMS must provide for privacy and security of student information. This is similar to the way the students' physical lockers provide a secure place for their belongings and dedicated facilities offer the privacy of restrooms and gym lockers/showers.

Today's classrooms should fulfill all requirements for traditional learning, all the way through to virtual classroom and online learning capabilities. This means that any type of media or live interaction can be at the fingertips of students and teachers alike, accessed via the web browser of their standard device. School sites should have media centers and makerspaces to accommodate small and larger work groups with access to technology. If you do an Internet search on features of a LMS, thousands of responses will be found ranging from the five main features to lists of hundreds of features.

For purposes of this book, the endeavor is not to exhaustively list every possible feature of an LMS but to list the requisite features and functionality to provide a robust platform for the development of T4c and its basic tenets of the 6Cs—which we'll analyze deeper.

Technical Requirements

Following is a list of technical capabilities of most LMSs currently in wide use.

Asynchronous Access

Asynchronous access to curriculum and instruction may be the most leveraged enhancement technology has to offer in the learning process. Since the beginning of time, when classes were taught in caves and around campfires, the synchronous interaction was the rule. There was *no* asynchronous learning method.

Gutenberg's press and the introduction of printed books and finally textbooks were the first evolution of a move toward asynchronous models, acknowledging that beyond reading the text as homework, 90 percent of all structured learning was still synchronous.

By using the LMS's homework and files posting/sharing mechanism, lesson plans can become entirely asynchronous, utilizing e-mail or messaging to communicate the availability and posting of homework or group work assignments.

Other factors make LMSs great for asynchronous learning including the following:

- recording of live meetings and then making them available via access to archives,
- links to Internet-based videos and online resources, and
- posting schedules and due dates in the calendars.

The inherent capability of recording video conferences, podcasts, and online lectures automatically enables any synchronous interaction to be asynchronous. In the author's most recent online learning course(s), every online interaction between the teacher and class (video conference, live chats, message boards, and audio conferences) were always recorded and made available to students to access asynchronously afterward. The only missing aspect might be a real-time question and answer interaction between teachers and students—which could surely be addressed asynchronously after the fact.

Social Media

Social media platforms (e.g., Facebook, Edmodo) that are limited to the school and class are great platforms for open sharing and commenting. They can also be a platform for lesson submission and messaging/

commenting between students and groups. These have the fundamental capabilities of user profiles, user pages, friends/contacts, daily postings/updates, calendar and scheduling, replies, and news.

An inherent advantage of these platforms is today's students understand exactly how these social media interactions should work. Tasks such as initial setup, profiles, security, and customization are similar and allow students to begin taking full advantage of the features and capabilities immediately.

Every teacher has already had the experience of having the students show the teachers how technology systems and "apps" are loaded and utilized. The high level of system security and protections built in to these platforms allow students to explore the learning system functionality just by "clicking-around" and figuring things out on their own.

Mobile Access/Multiplatform

One of the main stumbling blocks of technology initiatives in the previous decade was the 1-to-1 platform. Schools and districts spent millions on laptops and student tablet devices that, at best, provided rudimentary-level technology capability, and, at worse, made an unmanageable classroom distraction and rendered many computers a pile of unused technology in a broom closet.

Educational technology (Ed tech) done right should allow access to the district's LMS on any platform, anytime, anywhere. Students should be able to access classroom resources from Chromebooks, laptops, or their personal tablets, smartphones, and home devices. They all have web browser and application functionality and can provide access to 100 percent of LMS functionality. This assumes school-wide LAN and Wi-Fi infrastructure and secure access to the Internet. From there it becomes a policy decision.

Again, in years past, information technology (IT) directors wrestled with the concept of BYOD (bring your own device), and whether the district/site would "allow" non district-standard devices access to the Wi-Fi and Internet. Today, this is a dead issue. Every school/district *must* provide BYOD access, not only to teachers and students but also to guests and other users who might come on-site.

Customizable Reporting

The LMS must provide the teacher and system administrators the ability to monitor and audit logs of student and teacher activity on the system. These various logs should also allow customized reporting that can inform teachers about students' specific interactions with the system, such as number or time of downloads, postings, submissions, comments, replies, and other statistics valuable for classroom management and student auditing purposes.

Ultimately, these statistics and reports should feed data into the appropriate instructional and analytical systems to fully empower all systems with all available data and data types.

Teacher/Student/Classroom Associations/Privileges —Data Integration

The LMS should provide integration with student information systems to automatically configure relationships between teachers, their classes, and the students in the classes. The integration must be flexible to allow for multiple teachers in a class and granular access and read/write privileges that can be customized for teachers.

For instance, the LMS should automatically be configured to relate students and teachers to classes according to the master schedule, but it should also allow teachers to create work groups with team names and designated leaders of these subgroups. It should allow teachers to create profiles and permissions for students as leaders and/or auditors, monitors, or graders. The integration should also allow data, assessments, and reporting to pass back to the student information system automatically.

Electronic Resources Folder for Student and Parents

A "resource" folder can be made for each class or subject area to provide students with a central "clearinghouse" for all standardized resources such as digital video libraries, articles, and magazines for specific projects and research and various other examples of providing a central location for access to classroom and homework resources. By making these available to parents through parent "portal" access, parents can gain visibility into what's happening in their child's classroom and homework activities. One example is a teacher utilizing Google Classroom to upload resources for students and parents including writing samples and rubrics in a resource folder.

For a California regions project, a third-grade teacher has assigned his students group projects using Google Slides. The teacher appointed a leader for each group in charge of leading the group work and directing production activities and defining team "roles." They had to research their group's assigned region from an informational text and electronic resources folder and create a Google Slides presentation, adding pictures, audio narration, and video clips from the resources folder. This example uses the Google Classroom LMS capabilities for centralized resource access for students and parents, as well as the Google Slides application for creation, collaboration, and presentation practicum models. This example also implements the "explicitly assigned" leadership construct we'll discuss later.

Message Boards

Message boards are different from chat rooms. Where chat rooms tend to be in real time and informal, message boards are more structured to allow teachers to post prompts for students to reply to that include time stamps, activity logs, and user logs. The message boards should be able to be used within the delivery mode of the lesson context.

The LMSs should provide the teacher with logs in order to see when a user

- initiates a message;
- reads and comments on another user's message;
- replies to a comment on her original message; and
- uploads or downloads files.

The number of messages, comments, and replies posted should also be available to the teacher. The system should provide a report that shows these log statistics for each assignment, each section, and for the whole course for grading and assessment purposes. True integration between the LMS and the student information service (SIS; gradebook) would export lesson plan grades to the gradebook automatically.

Assignment Posting Grading/Assessment/Resubmission/Evaluation

Assignment posting is the ability of the teacher or staff person to post a homework or group work assignment for distribution to the students. The system should be able to track who downloads the assignment and when, in order to log receipt of the assignment by each student. It should also facilitate return submission of the assignment back into the system and include the ability to do a plagiarism test (e.g., Turnitin.com).

This is one area where LMS's assignment posting, grading, and resubmission prove their weight in gold. In *Next Practices: An Executive Guide for Education Decision Makers*, the authors posited that one-to-one projects were inherently flawed because they were technology oriented, meaning one device to one student. This is only focused on technology and accessibility. The authors reanointed the term to be a new technological capability of this assignment submission, grading, and resubmission process as the true one-to-one educational model—it's based on one-teacher, one-student. The capability of the LMS to achieve this highly iterative assignment model that allows multiple cycles of submission, review, revision, and resubmission, within a homework and grading cycle, to be a true technological advancement over traditional homework submission models.

For writing exercises, think about being able to discuss options for the best revision with the teacher before the final submission. This model is more like the real world, where a document or copy would be reviewed by multiple editors and reviewers, and multiple revisions might take place before final publication and/or distribution.

Calendar/Scheduling

Calendars are requisite features of an LMS, allowing the user to view infinite calendar views:

- Their own,
- Their classes' prompts, assignments, and due dates,
- Their college announcements and events,
- Other groups announcements and events,
- School-wide announcements and events, and
- District-wide announcements and events.

The calendar should include the school schedule, holidays, and other district dates of significance. It should serve as alerts and reminders for student's homework and project due dates. They might even be able to support each user's personal calendar and scheduling information such as birthdays and family vacations. Why not?

Assignment Submission/Validation (Plagiarism)

The system should have a secure process for students to upload (submit) their assignments back to the teacher into a folder where all the students' assignments are accumulated as well as checked for plagiarism.

From the teacher's standpoint, each submission should be time stamped and logged to the submitter to validate who submitted the work and when. The system should be able to note additional students who might have worked on the project as part of work groups or collaborative effort. The system should not be limited by number of submissions or submitters and must time stamp each individual submission with a unique identifier so that files do not overwrite or replace other files.

From the student's standpoint, the submission capability should allow for plain text up through document and even video formatted submissions. The teacher might be able to constrain file types for submissions, for instance, PDF documents only or all videos must be of a specific filetype.

Functional Requirements–Preferred

SKILL/CERTIFICATION TRACKING

Skill and/or certification tracking is a basic function of most LMSs today. This allows both integral as well as enterable skill/certification tracking mechanisms. These should be flexible enough to support site, district, as well as county office/state education skills/certification programs. At last (search) count, a search for "LMS with Certification Tracking" yielded 295 results. Browsing through this list demonstrates that skills/certification tracking is a top feature of LMS.

Part of certification tracking systems feature sets include the ability to track the certification number, expiry date, status, certification issuer, region, province or state, and certification agency of each certificate. This category and listings should be able to be configured and modified by the LMS administrators.

The skills/certification tracking should also feature a printing and storage function as well as the ability to export to other certification tracking systems that may need to be integrated with district, county or other state agencies.

GAMIFICATION

Gamification in the educational realm tends toward adding game design elements to existing curriculum. By adding gaming elements to curriculum, the teacher can improve student engagement through scoring, competition, and ease of usability. This is part of the Learning and Delivery Context in T4c development. Gamification elements include the following:

- Points/Scoring—Points and scoring allow the students to accumulate points that can be used for comparison and acquisition of milestones or awards.
- Badges/Prizes—Awards might be objective or subjective. They may be real, like certificates, medals, or trophies. They might be subjective like levels (novice, intermediate, advanced) or layers (white belt, blue belt, black belt).
- Pyramids/Leaderboards—Pyramids and/or leaderboards are used to enhance the competitive gaming elements by providing a public

display of performance. Students can see their scoring and progress in comparison to the other students in the class, or even between classes or between schools, or between districts. Why wouldn't an eighth-grade science class in California be able to compare their skills and capabilities against an eighth-grade science class in Tokyo?
- Performance Competition and Graphic Displays—These are similar to leaderboards. Dynamic displays of performance and competition might be displayed on the class web page or even the school marquee.
- Avatars—Avatars are alternate visual images of students within the class or school. Usually, they are chosen or created by the student but could easily be attached from the school SIS system or managed by the teacher. Avatars can be designed quite simply as a pictogram, illustration, or they could be animated, three-dimensional representations. Their main gamification element should be that they provide a unique identifier for the student and can be easily distinguished from other students and computer personalities within the game context.
- Teams—Once again, gamification can extend to collaborative models required for the work group. In the gamification environment, work groups become teams and can create and maintain their own profiles, avatars, skill sets, and personalities.

Video Conferencing

Virtually all LMSs support collaborative communications, the most fundamental being video conferencing or video chat. The relevant features should include all models and modes of classroom and leader-led delivery contexts.

In the traditional leader-led video conference, the teacher has predominant control over what is displayed on teach students view (browser window or device display). All the students can see the teacher and any number of displays or presentations the teacher may include in the curriculum delivery. The level of teacher control can be modified by administrators and teachers can control the views and capabilities of the students. For instance, the teacher should be able to control if students can see each other's camera views or if voice activation might bring their video to the forefront.

Audio conferences should allow chat rooms and the ability for the teacher to control whose voice can be heard in the conference. Similarly, a conference might support total equality within the group where participants can only control their own audio and video feeds.

COLLABORATION

Collaboration is one of the key elements in the development of critical thinking and group work models. For students to work together, an analytical and creative understanding of a topic is requisite. In order to facilitate collaboration, the student must have a basic understanding of the curriculum and the resultant lesson plan and assessment. The student *engenders* the subject matter to the point of being able to relate terms and factors to team members. Additionally, the students must have the basic proficiency of each of the tools and systems they will be using.

One of the first challenges in any implicit or explicit work group is "Who will be the leader?" And for a newer perspective that occurs at the T4c level, these questions can be entertained:

- Who should be the leader?
- Who's turn is it to be the leader?
- Pick your group's leader.
- Observe who emerges as the leader.

Leadership roles can be implicit or explicit. In fact, this concept within the collaborative model can also be a factor controlled by the developer as well as the teacher. Once this concept of managing the work group leadership construct is embraced, a higher-level of interpersonal communication skills are being addressed by the teacher. It is important to note that no matter the curriculum model or lesson plan, once the teacher determines the collaborative factors (if any), they then have the luxury to decide what, if any, higher-level interpersonal or leadership skills might be a point of focus in the delivery context of the lesson.

Leadership Constructs

Leadership constructs are models for designating or defining which student takes the leadership role. Five leadership constructs are at the determination of the teacher: (1) explicit assigned, (2) explicit determined, (3) implicit nondetermined, (4) equal partners, and (5) designated equal partners.

Explicit Assigned

In the *explicit assigned* construct, the teacher will explicitly assign the group leader for any variety of reasons as determined. The teacher should attempt to have all students take turns as leader in order to force a fundamental practicum in collaborative leadership.

Alternately, a teacher might designate the best leader for a project in order to ensure the best quality result based on the designee's natural leadership skills. Similar to picking the team captains who then select their individual team members, this construct tends to allow the teacher to favor a student, if not intentionally balanced. It also enables a scenario where the teacher picks the groups and then picks the leader of each group. This might be done simply for efficiency but also as a rotational responsibility model.

Explicit Determined

The *explicit determined* construct may occur once a work group is defined and the teacher either declares "Pick a leader" or designates a lead. Obviously, an infinite number of variations of the outcome of this type of leadership construct occur based on the number of individuals in the work group and their individual personalities and traits. The likelihood of any individual student declaring themselves leader is just as common as individual students designating whom should lead based on whatever circumstances or phenomenon may be relevant to the situation.

Ultimately, leadership is determined to be designated in the construct. The teacher has the option as well to provide a model for determining the leaders. A democratic "voting" model might be introduced, or alternately the teacher may require individuals to lobby and convince the group to be the leaders. Different tasks or awards may be used to incent team members to compete for the leadership role.

Implicit Nondetermined

In the *implicit nondetermined* construct, the teacher does not give guidelines as part of the work group instructions. It can be part of the teacher's analysis to see which students emerge as leaders within small designated work groups. It becomes a management factor of the teachers to rotate the designation—or nondesignation—of the work group leader to help develop and refine leadership skills for each student by manipulating the leadership construct.

Equal Partners

An *equal partners* construct is a flexible option wherein the teacher defines the work groups, or allows them to define themselves, and does not explicitly designate a leader or a need for a leader in the lesson context. Once again, the teacher can analyze how the students work together as a group and observe which student emerges as a leader or task master.

DESIGNATED EQUAL PARTNERS

The tendency for some to seek leadership roles might be cause for the teacher to declare that students are *equal partners* in a particular work group or lesson context. This declaration could be done to specifically inhibit the actions of some that have historically imposed their leadership upon work groups and allow others to take on balanced responsibility. However, this type of shared responsibility requires equal consideration from each party with the risk of some parties not contributing equally. A balanced grading system might be used to distribute the grade equally among the members regardless of the actual amount of work performed and a method to incent equal effort.

Collaboration Spaces

Collaboration spaces, much like the well-known "makerspaces" are learning areas that provide tools for individual students or small work groups to work collaboratively and to make or create projects. This may include robotics spaces, coding labs, and video production studios.

Robotics labs typically require some workbench-type spaces that allow for assembly and construction of robotics components as well as computing capability to facilitate coding for the robotic systems.

Coding labs might be a small group of laptops or Chromebooks with access to a coding or development application platform that all students can work on collaboratively, test, and demonstrate the capabilities of the coded applications.

Video production studios are typically a dedicated space with higher quality video cameras and video production workstation and software. These spaces usually feature a production set for hosts and guests, backed by a green screen to allow video production software to overlay background images into the video backdrop.

Additional leadership constructs can occur in these collaboration spaces and differently skilled individuals may be more inclined to take responsibility because of specific skill sets and experience in robotics, coding, and/or video and media production. Some of these other leadership constructs might include project manager, lead programmer, set director, and video editor and producer.

Messaging Standards

Messaging boards and "old-school" bulletin board services (BBS) are possibly the oldest technology applications for collaboration. The ability to write, store, and forward written communications allow groups of people to read and view these messages and then reply either privately or to the group/subgroup.

Messaging boards in LMSs also have additional capabilities that foster collaboration as well as assessment. By having time stamps, the system and teacher can schedule postings and due dates, and audit by the second who posts or submits on time. Additionally, statistics regarding elapsed times between postings and number of postings, the teacher can see how much time is expended on the system. By logging replies, the system can log and the teacher can assign a quota for postings as well as number of replies. For example, the assignment might include the following:

1. Responding to a prompt on the assignment board
2. Reading at least three other student's responses
3. And reviewing and replying to at least three separate postings

Working in these types of collaboration groups present their own timing and logistical challenges. Students that wait until the deadline before submitting, don't have their postings available for others to review, and therefore might not be able to get enough responses to their postings. They do however have the full classes' worth of another student's posting to choose from. While early posters might have to wait and log in repeatedly to fulfill the number of interactions required.

Deadlines for message comments and replies should be one or two more days beyond the initial posting date to allow for more interactions. Of course, the teacher can also make posting and comment/replies under a very tight schedule in order to keep the synchronicity of events closer. Guidelines should be provided to structure the types of postings, grammar rules, plagiarism, constructive criticism, inappropriate postings, and so on.

Modes of Collaboration

As varied as the leadership constructs, modes of collaboration are also infinite, and allow the size and type of the work group to provide practical constraints on the collaborative modes for a lesson plan. Keep in mind, any particular curriculum or lesson plan can be implemented with varying degrees of collaboration—whether synchronous or asynchronous, remote or face-to-face.

In our book *Vision: The First Critical Step in Developing a Strategy for Education Technology*, the authors discuss learning spaces and how flexible learning spaces and various models of interaction support various collaborative models. These discussions mostly originate from David

Thornburg's analysis of learning spaces in his book *From the Campfire to the Holodeck* (Thornburg 2013; Holtthink 2014).

Here's a look at the primary collaboration models associated with these four learning spaces described first by Thornburg. Expanded for collaboration from *Vision*:

CAVE

Here you: withdraw from the noise of the classroom to be alone with your thoughts and reflection. A place to explore questions and make connections.
Think: a beanbag enclosed by bookshelves.
Collaboration: a two- or three-person (intimate) work group. A group that might have two evenly skilled members or two members with diverse skills.
For example,

- two SMEs;
- one instructional designer and one SME; and
- one writer, one director, and one talent.

CAMPFIRE

Here you: share stories, exchange ideas, and allow the group to build on each other's ideas.
Think: a group brainstorming about ways to advertise their product to the community.
Collaboration: a group of three- to some number less than ten; a small group with diverse skills and a designated leader; a small group of peers working toward a common objective, such as a scavenger hunt or canoe trip.
For example,

- a basketball team with a coach, five starters, and four bench players;
- a newspaper production crew such as reporters, layout designers, editors, and publisher; or
- a wagon train with a driver, a cook, a cowboy, and a family.

SANDBOX

Here you: play, prototype, and experiment without worrying about mess, water, or damaging surfaces.
Think: testing your bridge design to see if it can support the weight of a toy car.

Collaboration: This is another small group exercise but more based on the concept of experimenting and testing rather than planning and executing. This experimenting and testing phase might be part of a larger project, to determine the course for execution.

For example,

- an experimental phase of a robotics competition to determine the most effective defense from an attacking robot;
- a subgroup of SMEs tasked with developing a standards-based curriculum for a lesson plan; or
- splitting a team of structural engineers into subgroups to build competing bridge designs out of toothpicks in order to validate design strength.

Watering Hole

Here you: come together to exchange ideas and cross-pollinate.

Think: a student learning programming and a student learning to dance sharing ideas about the creative process while having a coffee.

Collaboration: This is small and intimate interactions occurring around others, with more free-form mixing. Consider talking to coworkers at the food service bars at an all-you-can-eat buffet or interactions with strangers at the DMV line.

For example,

- Giving each student an individualized scavenger hunt application where they will and/or must interact with others to gain knowledge or get help; or
- posting a homework assignment on the message board where students can propose solutions to a prompt, read others' responses, and add ideas and critiques to each other's solutions.

Source: "Caves, Campfires, and Watering Holes," Core Education, http://www.core-ed.org/sites/events.core-ed.org/files/Caves-campfires-wateringholes.pdf.

Performance Models

Another key critical thinking skill and alternative mode of collaboration in the interpersonal communications space are performance skills and models. It is common knowledge that many people are more fearful of public speaking than even death, yet what is done at grade levels to address this fear? By integrating performance models into the higher-level activities in a lesson plan, each student is encouraged and/or required to do some performance or demonstration of understanding.

Performance models can be individual or collaborative, such as a monologue, or a skit. Something as simple as doing weather reports in the context of a news broadcast is a perfect example where a small group would need a director/producer (off camera), talent (on camera), and production assistant, video/audio, and postproduction.

Meld into that marketing and assessment activities and the performance models within the lesson plans can take many forms: from the basic performances themselves, to interview and news broadcast formats, to b-roll recording and behind-the-scenes reporting, to having each team member present their works to the classroom for the final qualitative assessment. Performance-based lesson plans can be as simple as an oral report or as complex as a mock trial. They could be one-day individual assignments or could be a whole section or semester.

CONTENT DEVELOPMENT PLATFORM

The content development platform might be an integrated part of the LMS, but the likelihood of this is decreased if the district has a centralized or core team of instructional designers/developers. We'll discuss the differences in these and other roles within the content development spectrum in-depth in later chapters.

For this part of the discussion related to content development platform systems and features it is important to note that if these platforms haven't been formally adopted for these roles, then the associated district development standards probably also don't exist. What are these standards we're speaking of? Each school or district must have some standards for curriculum development such as acceptable/licensed applications for the following:

- multimedia presentations (slide show),
- graphic design and layout,
- digital imaging and illustration,
- video production,
- journalism and publishing, and
- web-page development.

Additionally, standards might also provide guidelines for these:

- color schemes and palette;
- fonts and styles;

- use of logos and templates for disciplines (math backgrounds and templates for graphs, formulas, animations); and
- other district curriculum to be used as standard video content.

For instance, one district might call for all schools to have their school website reflective of the colors of each site and their associated mascots. An alternate example might be a district website that has its own standardized color scheme and design layout, and this color palette and layout is used for each school consistently.

Electronic Resources

Many districts subscribe to digital services for educational content for use in the classroom. These services should be able to be integrated with the curriculum development platform. For instance, streaming videos should be able to be linked via HTML as opposed to having to download and store high-definition video online. Once again, teacher familiarity with these services is critical if they're to be leveraged for instruction. This area is so diverse that it will suffice to say, T4c allows the integration and augmentation of any existing digital resource into the lesson and delivery context.

Content Development Services

Do one Google search for "instructional content development," and you'll get a bevy of domestic and an even greater abundance of overseas content development firms. So much that you'll be sorry you did the search in the first place. They'll be e-mailing and connecting with you on social media.

There will be tens, if not hundreds of firms that would love to contract with your school to do all the instructional design and development you could ever dream of—or have a nightmare about how much it would cost. Obviously, if the best way to implement T4c was to contract it out overseas, then this book would be about one chapter long.

Any instructional development house worth their salt would have the answers to every question posed in the chapters of this book—and there are many. They will claim to already have standards for development, navigation, color palates, themes, and even access to curriculum. But the other point is that they do not know each school's demographics, culture, values, and students—they do not know a school's teachers and students.

In-House Content Development

Most of the remainder of this book is about this subject—in-house development. Realistically, the only way a district can make a significant move to T4c is through in-house content development. It's not unlike Machiavelli's assertion that the best soldiers are borne of the country (city-state) for which they fight. Mercenaries do so for the gold, and they are the first to lose their loyalty in the face of destruction.

The educational parallel is not so dramatic, but any school or district can pay for these types of development resources. It can also be asserted that there is no way the cost of this development can be less than utilizing internal talent within the organization; and besides, these resources would have a personal investment in the quality of the curriculum they develop. Their vested interest is the success and achievement of the students for which they develop said content.

This in-house capability is a team of resources that might be distributed between the district office (ed services) and the sites, but their loyalty and understanding of their school and community is an important aspect of their design and development aptitude.

This team must be "purpose-built." We're talking about a T4c program manager, instructional designers, and SMEs, designing and developing according to a strategic plan and scope of work. Not a repurposed TOSA and a bunch of "tech" teachers. No one person could hope to be a sole T4c content developer for a whole district.

So, as administrators dealing with this question about how to raise the quality and standards for curriculum, start thinking about how to organize and justify these resources. The following chapters will provide a strategic plan for T4c mastery and innovation!

Designers/Developers/SMEs

When thinking about this in-house development team, think also about the difference between instructional designers/developers and SMEs. Once considered, it should be clear that, the SMEs are more likely teachers and site-based resources, while the designers/developers might likely be district-based resources. But this is not a rule; it's just the way resources naturally align and occur in the educational structure.

Designers are more on the standards side of the development process. They are testing, developing the templates, tools, standard formats, and standards for T4c components. Developers are the resources implementing the designs and standards using content gathered from the adopted curriculum basis, the Common Core State Standards (CCSS) and the SMEs. Developers are full-blown T4c authors. The SMEs would be focused on grade-level and/or discipline-based curriculum.

STANDARDS FOR DEVELOPMENT

The final key technology feature to discuss, which has been alluded to many times without details, thus far, is the need for standards. The funny thing is, standards are not technologies in and of themselves. Standards exist to guide and align technologies and curriculum. There's nothing worse than having adopted curriculum that isn't consistent across schools and grade levels. Many educators have seen examples of "We're using this tool for this application, and this tool for that, and they really don't integrate that well."

The issues that must be considered before addressing these standards are more related to *who* will develop these standards; and once developed, *who* will maintain and enforce these standards? Are they the same people? Does that even make sense?

One of these factors is the many layers and complexities of these considerations regarding technology and standards. There isn't one way of doing things in the IT world and funny enough, this book will not deal with any standards of the IT world. Those standards are already defined and implemented. The standards for IT, like cabling, equipment, connectivity, and support have been standardized and are in practice in most schools already, hopefully, in a state of functionality that supports all instructional endeavors and initiatives. If your school isn't there yet, put this book down and read the author's last two books on ed tech strategic planning (Vidal and Casey, *Vision* 2014) and ed tech project management (Vidal 2018). These books will help educators identify and plan from your school's technology infrastructure needs (technology strategic planning) and then help you plan and manage each project (project planning and project management). These books address these areas ad nauseum and provide a roadmap and implementation guide to educational technology infrastructure and management.

This book assumes that all things IT are already in place and in operation. So what standards are relevant when talking about the educational technology realm?

CHAPTER 3—ACTION ITEMS

1. *Assess your school's standards and use of:*
    a. *Learning Management Systems*
        Has your school or district standardized on a LMS?
        Is there a comprehensive professional development (PD) program to support teacher implementation of the LMS?

b. *Collaboration Platforms*

Has your school or district standardized on a collaboration platform?

Is there a comprehensive PD program to support teacher implementation of the collaboration platform?

c. *Content Development Platforms*

Has your school or district standardized on a content development platform?

Is there a comprehensive PD program to support teacher implementation of the content development platform?

d. *Content Development Standards*

Has your school or district developed standards for curriculum and content development?

Is there a comprehensive PD program to support teacher innovation based on the content development standards?

Chapter 4

A New Name for Redefinition

In an effort to discuss the standardized development of curriculum a series of questions are manifested:

- Who will lead this effort?
- Who will do the development?
- What standards will they follow?
- What platform will they use?
- Who are the subject matter experts (SMEs)?
- Who are the grade-level representatives?

Let's address these questions one at a time.

Who will lead this development?
Someone must take the lead in advocating and sponsoring this development. It is a requisite that this person champion the effort from a position of impact. What does that mean? It means that an individual teacher likely cannot lead this development beyond a simple proof-of-concept, or individual lesson series.

It means that someone at the district level that understands the concept of the SAMR model (substitution, augmentation, modification, and redefinition), where their district staff and technology is in relation to the infrastructure, has the authority and ability to engage staff, and develop a strategic plan to implement Tier 4 Curriculum (T4c), must take the lead and make the initiative real. Who is this in your district? Examining these requirements one at a time, the reader will see what and/whom that person might be.

The person that could fulfill this role might be a current district administrator or staff member that meets the following:

1. Understands the SAMR model and recognizes its value and benefit to the district.
   This might be the assistant superintendent of instruction or someone within that department that has the technical acumen to define the needs and standards that justify a district-wide T4c initiative.

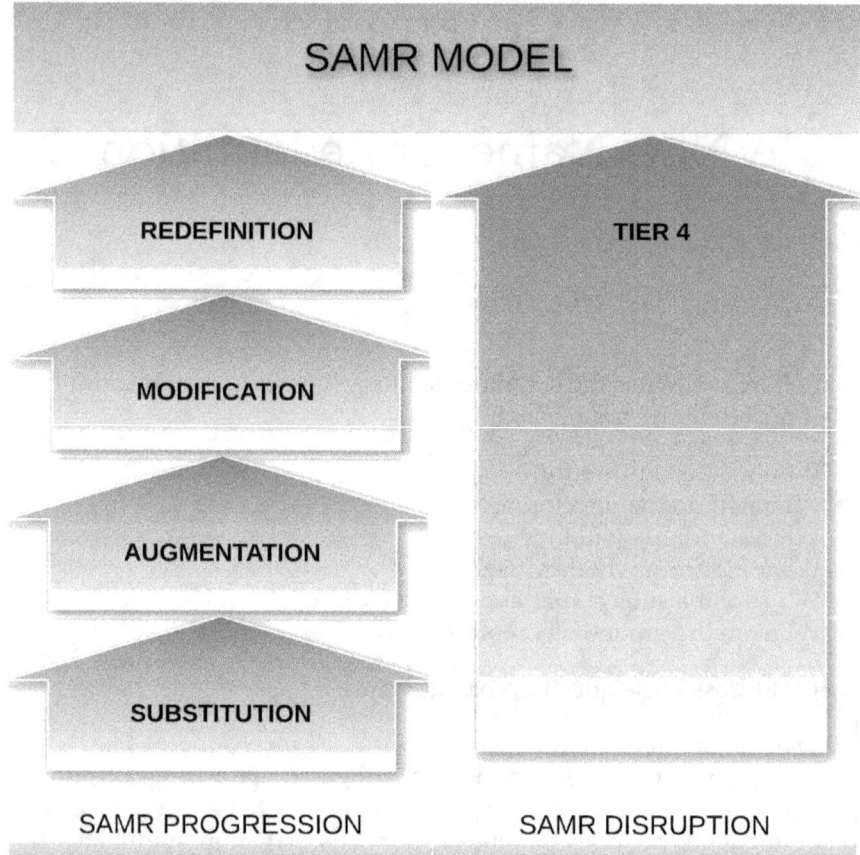

Figure 4.1. SAMR Disruption

2. Understands the district technology infrastructure and its ability to support the proposed efforts.

    This person is likely more of an information technology (IT) director–type person, or an IT infrastructure staff member. Rarely do the instructional support staff members have this intimate understanding for district-wide technology infrastructure and what future technology initiatives and standards might be in relation to the development and delivery of T4c.
3. Has the ability and authority to engage staff and/or create new staff positions within the organization.

    Once again, this is a cabinet-level administrator that can propose and impact the departmental staffing at the planning level and define the staffing requirements at the operational level.

4. The ability to initiate the development of a strategic plan to implement T4c.

   This is again a director or higher-level member of the instructional staff that understands T4c (top of the SAMR model) and can affect a strategic planning endeavor in order to justify the work roles and additional head count to support the T4c development effort.

Keep in mind, this resource or these resources may be directly related to district size. The number of students and schools will directly impact the size of this department. Additional factors include the implementation timeline for the T4c development effort. If leadership identifies this need as urgent or immediate, a full staff might be necessary to plan, lead, and staff this endeavor. Alternately, a small district might just need one T4c TOSA(teacher on special assignment) to lead a mentoring/coaching model for T4c development.

In the book, *Project Management in the Ed Tech Era* (Vidal 2018), the author wrote about how every project must have a name. The name makes the project real; it gives it sanction. When the school superintendent starts calling a project by name, it's sanctioned from the top. Once given funding and assigned resources, the project is real. Without these three items (name, funding, and resources), there is no initiative or project.

It's also relevant to note that the superintendent cannot be the lead; it must be someone on the instructional side of the house, like the assistant superintendent of instruction. But even this person will likely not be the leader of the initiative—or lead developer; these resources will likely report to this department. Then, who? That brings us to the next question:

Who will do this development? Who is the execution resource?

This question brings on thoughts of instructional designers, instructional services staff or TOSAs. Most districts have staff with these titles or something similar, but ask yourself—are these staff members ready to take on this task and responsibilities over and above their current duties? Do they have the skills to lead this type of development initiative—what, more questions?

For example, who will explain the T4c concept to the development staff? It obviously must be someone who's read this book. Once again, is the person who might read and understand the concept of T4c the same person who can get the sanction, create the plan, hire the resources, and provide their professional development? What training will they need to be able to do this development? Sorry, we're asking more questions than we're answering. Let's continue.

What standards will they follow?

In this question we're not referring to Common Core State Standards (CCSS), we're referring to district or school standards for curriculum development. A school can't have a development team without having standards about how curriculum should look, feel, and operate. For example, a simple standard might be that slide decks are made in MS PowerPoint (or alternately Google Slides) and that each school has a set of slide masters and backgrounds consistent for all curriculum for that school. But beyond the platform, what about standards for the following?

- Curriculum outline
- Navigation methods (do they use arrows, NEXT buttons, or something more detailed and flexible?
- Quiz and testing formats
- Standards for video and audio production and use
- And so on

By implementing standards for curriculum development, teachers will be empowered to embrace the new curriculum because they will know and understand how it will work, and that it will achieve the basic requirements of the lesson plan. Funny, that if you Google "curriculum development standards," you'll find state and federal standards, but you probably won't find anything specific for how a PowerPoint slide deck for Secondary Social Studies should look, feel, and operate.

The standards are specific to the school/district and will also be likely dictated by the platform(s) used, such as PowerPoint, Google Slides, or a platform integrated with a learning management system (LMS) like Blackboard. Suffice it to say that your school/district must develop its own standards for curriculum development.

What platform will they use?

A quick Google search of curriculum development software will yield an endless list of software and tools, so where to start with this question? As alluded to earlier, the LMS may have a development platform integrated within its feature set. The good news is that this makes the decision about which development platform easy. The bad news is that the integrated development tools might not be as robust as the non-LMS-based tools available.

For instance, video or animation creation tools probably aren't part of one of these integrated toolkits. So, the question about which development platform will be used (licensed) may be complicated by the standards that have been defined and the software licensed. It's plausible that in the early stages, the built-in features of the LMS are used by the development team, but then after some time, more robust tools are added to the suite for more compelling or specific curriculum components. For instance, maybe the built-in platform is used for standard curriculum but then enhanced with customized animations or graphics that are developed on another platform and then integrated into the lesson plan.

Who are the subject matter experts (SMEs)?

Here's another trick question. You might think that curriculum that already exists in the state standards doesn't require an SME, but once the developer/designer wants to go beyond the state standards, how will they validate the curriculum without an SME? Luckily, this is simply a matter of making a list.

This is an undertaking in itself, but it's likely that most schools/districts have a large selection of SMEs currently on the teaching staff. This list becomes part of an organized SME database that is referenced in the instructional design process. This list must be maintained by a district instructional resource and it also can become a guide to allow teachers to become SMEs for a leadership position and possibly a stipend.

For example, by volunteering to become an SME for grade-level curriculum review, that teacher might be at the top of the list to become a mentor or development resource in the future.

Who are the grade-level representatives?

Like the last question, at least we're seeing that these resources are likely in-house. It's also very likely that these staff members are already identified on another basis—like department chairs or grade-level leads. It's simply a matter of identifying these resources and providing the respective PD for this development, along with their interest in taking on these responsibilities.

Clearly, it's a big undertaking. It hasn't even completely taken hold in higher education, but it's a phenomenon in most educational institutions and communities. Any visit to a K–12 education conference will highlight real classroom examples of the most impressive T4c in action at all grade levels and in all socioeconomic settings.

The follow-up question for any of these highlighted examples is this: has this development model been adopted as a standard for the whole curriculum/site/district? Clearly, these greatest examples of T4c were not planned according to this development process, but they demonstrate the requisite attributes, and outcomes engendered in T4c.

T4c encompasses the concept of digital everything, synchronous and asynchronous lesson delivery, posting, submission, collaboration, discussion, assessment, cumulation, aggregation, and ultimately achievement in testing. T4c empowers the individual teacher to customize and optimize

Table 4.1. Attributes and Outcomes of Tier 4 Curriculum

Attributes of T4c	Alignment with CCSS
	Utilizes LMS features
	Utilizes technology (not paper based)
	Cognitive factors
	Involves critical thinking skills (Bloom's)
	Leverages collaboration opportunities
Outcomes of T4c	Demonstration of cognitive factors
	Achievement of standards testing
	Technology proficiency
	Critical thinking–advanced deduction, synthesis, evaluation, creation
	Collaboration / leadership skills / performance skills.

the lesson/curriculum to the needs of the class and even the individual student. Because everything is digital, from content to interaction, everything can be done remotely—except for shaking hands!

T4c's model of inherent collaboration allows the teacher to balance group work while enforcing accountability and individual assessment/achievement. How? By requiring aspects of the submission/interaction to be measured and tracked via the LMS. The integral capability of the LMS to provide individualized time stamps and history of the student's interaction with the curriculum and his or her peers within the LMS platform fundamentally renders all activities subject to forensic scrutiny.

TIER 4 CURRICULUM—THE 6CS

The 6C development process is nothing more than a checkoff list that can help any teacher or T4c developer plan a T4c project. The process provides the inquiry methodology any teacher or instructional designer can follow to develop T4c that can engage individual students or collaboration groups. The concept of T4c requires a clear understanding of the SAMR model but taken to the furthest progression.

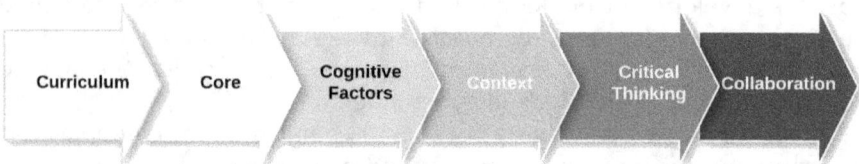

Figure 4.2. The 6Cs of Tier 4 Curriculum Development

Once the concept and capabilities of the "redefinition" layer are understood, the model forgets the preliminary phases of SAMR—substitution, augmentation, and modification—and realizes that "redefinition" should really be a target of development standards rather than a destination achieved via a journey—a long and laborious one, at that. Once the journey has been made, and the concepts, features, and functions of "redefinition" are defined and mapped out, the name "redefinition" in and of itself, makes no sense, thus Tier 4 curriculum—T4c.

We'll do a deep dive into each of the 6Cs further in the next chapter, but here's the gist of it.

1. Curriculum

The 6C process starts with curriculum—or existing content and lesson plans. Typically, each district/site has a base of electronic curriculum to start with. It may be easiest to start with lessons and plans that are already in existence, otherwise the process of curriculum development will have to precede the process of T4c development.

That's not to say that the current curriculum is always the best. Your school's current curriculum is probably dated. Whether or not it has actually become obsolete is to be determined, so the assessment of the current curriculum base available at the district is warranted by the T4c development team.

It's also likely that the school's current base of curriculum is a mixture of this service and that collection of resources—some current, some not. The planning for development must be prioritized to address the most urgent needs, balanced by what can readily be prioritized.

2. Core—CCSS

CCSS are a matter of alignment and compliance. Presumably that "existing" curriculum discussed in item 1 already aligns with CCSS. It may need to be updated or revised as part of the planning and development process, but it must be recognized that fundamental content development and CCSS alignment should be a given in the T4c development process.

If there is also a need to assess if the current curriculum is up to state standards, here the reader will encounter another obstacle to diving directly into development. Does the current curriculum need to be first revised to reflect new state standards, or can the T4c development team leverage the existing curriculum and turn it directly into T4c that also complies with state standards in one effort instead of two?

3. Cognitive Factors

The cognitive factors are the fundamental facts and details of basic comprehension of the lesson. The cognitive factors may be the check-off items that will likely appear in state tests. It should be easy for the T4c developers to identify the cognitive factors of any lesson plan. These cognitive factors should also be evaluated for compliance with the newest state standards and the most recent interpretation of history.

4. Context

Context provides the teacher an idea of how the lesson might be taught, in terms of a real-world example or possibly an imaginary/conceptual scenario. Additionally, the delivery scenario provides an example or concept of what technologies and model might be used in implementation and "delivery" of the lesson plan, and the work or group work the students shall use to absorb and respond to the lesson.

(A) LESSON CONTEXT

The lesson context provides the teacher with a fundamental concept of how to present the lesson to the class. Using a behaviorist approach, the lesson context might leverage a real-world scenario that students must participate in to experience the lesson.

(B) DELIVERY CONTEXT

The delivery context provides the teacher with a standard method or model for delivery of the lesson using technology. This might include using a video to establish a lesson scenario and a tour bus or news report to establish the delivery context.

5. Critical Thinking

The critical thinking stage is where the designer plans how to engage the students' higher-level skills of analysis, evaluation, and formulation/creation.

6. Collaboration

Finally, the collaboration component encourages the designer and the implementer to explore how individuals, groups, and the class as a whole might interact for that lesson.

As discussed in the development process, the reader must also recognize that various aspects of the development process may dictate how they are developed and implemented. There are various subcategories of user: developer, designer, implementer, and teacher.

DEVELOPMENT RESOURCES

Developer

The developer designation will be used as all-encompassing in terms of both development and implementation of the curriculum. The developer might be a district resource, a site resource, or an individual teacher. The developer in this context is the person creating the curriculum and lesson plan either from current curriculum or developing the components and the plan for delivery. For example, an individual teacher, taking district curriculum and developing a slide deck for a language arts lesson plan, may decide to design the curriculum to be viewed as a classroom lecture delivered by the teacher (developer in this case) and a homework writing project for completion by the student. In this example, the teacher is the designer, developer, and implementer.

So, in this respect, anyone can be a developer. As such, the developer must adhere to state as well as district standards, and if they are more or less stand-alone resources (meaning they aren't part of a bigger team of designers/developers) then there must be a team or designee assigned to review the curriculum and ensure the adherence to these standards—or in many cases, the development and documentation of standards.

Designer

The designer designation will be used to discuss a resource strictly scoped for developing the content for T4c. These might be PowerPoint slides, videos, or other curriculum support media to be used by implementers and teachers. Designers may be a core group of curriculum developers who are not SMEs or teachers. Their scope might be specifically to take subject matter in the form of existing curriculum and converting them to PowerPoint, slides, infographics, or video snippets.

An example of an instructional designer is a district media resource teacher whose primary purpose for a particular school year would be to create interactive slide decks of the recently adopted electronic resources. Engaging one or a small group of dedicated instructional designers to create T4c in a concerted effort is a good way to ensure that lesson plans are developed based on a standard look and feel, alignment to state standards, and to have a consistent navigation and interaction with the end users.

As a designated designer, this resource or team should be tasked with developing curriculum according to these standards, documenting the standards for all team resources, which should include maintaining the central documentation store for these standards and the resulting curricula.

Subject Matter Experts

SMEs are those innovative teachers and coordinators who have specific needs for curriculum, are experts in the content, and have vision for the 6Cs but don't have the time necessary to do their own T4c development. SMEs are likely distributed throughout the sites at all grade levels. One important factor about SMEs is that they are not only requestors and participants in the development process, but they are also consumers of the lessons and artifacts produced. Thus, the SMEs, over time, become not only experts in their discipline but also in the T4c development and implementation.

Implementer

Implementers will be used to discuss site resources planning and using curriculum for classroom use. Teachers may be implementers when they are engaged in rolling out T4c to more than their own classrooms—for instance, for their whole grade level. A teacher assigned the task of curriculum development will likely be afforded the opportunity to share the curriculum lesson to others in the department. Part of this implementer role then may also include training, and/or train-the-trainer type models for expanding the reach and use of the T4c.

Teacher

The teacher designation for the T4c discussion refers to individual teachers using curriculum and planning for an individual classroom lesson. Teachers and implementers can develop content.

CHAPTER 4—ACTION ITEMS

1. *Assess your school's potential to assemble a T4c development team*
   Review your district's instructional and IT staff to see if there is a nascent technology innovator or champion in the midst.

2. *Identify potential development resources who could be:*
   a. *Developers*

   Developers can handle all tasks in the T4c development process. Developers may also be project or program managers in a larger team.

   b. *Designers*

   Designers are more focused on the content development tools and their standardized use. They would tend to work with SMEs. Designers will be masters of the content development standards and platforms.

   c. *SMEs*

   SMEs can come from anywhere in the district, although they're most likely teachers and team leaders. Since they will be implementers they become both producers and consumers of the T4c product.

Chapter 5

The 6C Development Process

CURRICULUM

Curriculum can come from anywhere. Most schools currently have adopted curriculum that already aligns with Common Core State Standards (CCSS). The question becomes who will develop the Tier 4 curriculum (T4c)? Is this a grade-level effort at each school or at the district-level? Should district-standard curriculum be developed by district curriculum staff, teachers on special assignment (TOSAs), or allow individual teachers to develop these on their own?

This discussion raises so many questions about training, standards, implementation, and professional development that it should be suggested that development can happen at all levels: grade-level site, grade-level district, district, and individual teacher. Later chapters in this book will explore a variety of models based on organic development to district developed resources.

There is a model that allows all these options to be pursued, and once curriculum has been developed, it is funneled through an approval process for compliance to standards and adopted at the district level as "district-approved" T4c.

CORE

Alignment with CCSS is requisite for any new curriculum development. This should already be done in the case of adopted curriculum, but new development of any T4c should be timely and up to date with CCSS with a look to the future. Not that the developer can predict changes in future standards but to follow the trend of state standards is to imply an implicit understanding of the basis of the standards to guide development.

Additionally, as curriculum is developed and implemented, a process of revision and version control should be implemented. For example, a lesson plan for a tenth-grade language arts prompt might also be revised for use in a tenth-grade social sciences lesson. Upon revision, both versions of the lesson plan would now be available in the curriculum base.

The objective of common core alignment is as pragmatic as "the student must learn what will be in the standards test." It is most likely that the fundamental (core) competencies defined in most CCSS standards are demonstrated in the cognitive realm; that means to say, the assessment of achievement in common core alignment are the test results.

COGNITIVE FACTORS

The cognitive factors for T4c are the salient points that students must understand and demonstrate as objectives for the lesson. Cognitive factors should be identified early in the development process and revisited throughout to provide a continuous check that the lesson holds close to the standard test requirements while also complementing overall understanding of the subject matter.

Bloom's taxonomy enters into every discussion of cognition and critical thinking, specifically of the cognitive domain. Commonly depicted as a pyramid of decreasing size and scale moving up the model, an alternate view is to depict the model as an inverted pyramid to reflect the depth of understanding and comprehension at the highest levels of the model. Where evaluation and creation are demonstrative and performance activities require the student to evince their depth of comprehension, context and relevance in relation to a lesson plan.

This most pragmatic and cynical viewpoint is tempered by the concept that the cognitive factors are the "salient" points of any lesson plan—the student must learn what he needs to learn.

For example, in a study of third-grade biomes, the student should be able to list each and write a general explanation of the biome characteristics. At the application level, the student can verbally discuss, demonstrate, or explain in a lecture or speech the relationship between the biomes and how they rely on each other.

Understanding versus Demonstrating

To reinforce the cognitive factors using the term understanding is not quantifiable.

Understanding attunes to comprehension and the ability to grasp the premise or point of the lesson, fundamentally—layer 2 of Bloom's

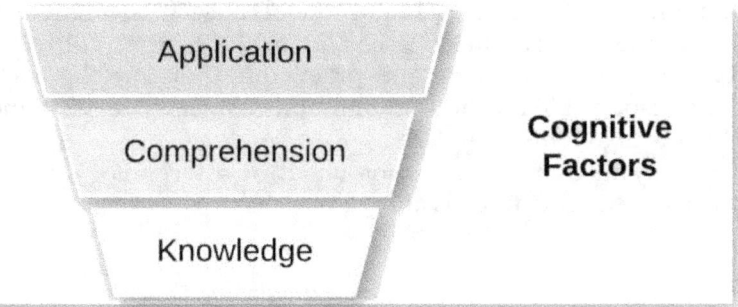

Figure 5.1. Cognitive Factors of Bloom's Taxonomy

taxonomy—but it doesn't attest to the true understanding or relevance, proportion, or application, the next step up the model and the top of the cognitive layers of the model.

A simple multiple-choice test or question/answer quiz can attest to the understanding and basic comprehension of a cognitive factor within a lesson. The application requires the student to demonstrate understanding of the use of the factor within the context of the lesson.

Regarding the development of T4c, the cognitive factors then become the "named" items addressed in the lesson—they are the answers to the questions that will appear in the standardized tests. It should also be considered how critical thinking exercises at the higher level of Bloom's taxonomy can reinforce the cognitive factors. For example, if the lesson plan of the Gettysburg Address includes a narrative describing the weather on that November date in 1863, the fact that it was cold and blustery might help the student remember the date.

Bloom's Taxonomy of Cognitive Objectives and T4c

The bottom three layers of Bloom's taxonomy of the cognitive realm directly relates to T4c for cognitive factors. For T4c development, the creator must identify the key factors that will encompass the fundamental data relevant to the lesson—the names, time periods, geographies, governments of a history lesson for instance.

In the endeavor to focus on critical thinking aspects of the lesson, the developer must not lose focus of the cognitive factors. These factors will tend to become important when standardized testing comes around. Additionally, high-level application of the lesson could be *diminished* by invalid data or misunderstanding of facts.

The cognitive factors become the core of the lesson plan while the delivery and practicum of the lesson become the core of the critical thinking aspects. This is important because it demonstrates that no matter the curriculum or lesson plan, the teacher still has complete control over the delivery and practicum; therefore the teacher is entirely responsible for the students' ability to achieve the higher-level of Bloom's taxonomy.

So, any thought or discussion about how technology can replace the teacher in the classroom is absurd.

CONTEXT

As described earlier, in the digital realm of education technology, the context of the lesson plan is two-fold:

- The *lesson context* is the "learning scenario"—or what is the sample scenario and circumstances of the learning event?
- The *delivery context* is the method and mode of delivery, requirements, body of work, and assessment—how students will receive, execute, submit, and assess the lesson.

Table 5.1. Learning Contexts and Delivery Contexts

Curriculum	Lesson Context	Delivery Context
Science/Biomes	Students are world explorers throughout various time periods	Using Google Maps and streaming videos to experience biomes
History/American Revolution	Students are colonialists and/or British politicians	News reporting crew as delivery using copy writing, layout, editing, publication
English/Language Arts	Students describe elements of the story or skill focus (e.g., theme of a story) using interactive LMS like Prezi or PowToons to display their understanding of the text	Students include examples of text evidence in presentation with visual animations, oral recordings, video recordings, text boxes, screenshots of the texts, pictures, etc.
Math/Area	Students are architects	Using Google Draw to display square footage of a dream home they create. Group collaboration by having students create different features of a home and aspects of creation

The great news about the context is that the teacher has partial control of the lesson context and full control of the delivery context—meaning that the teacher is never locked out of the implementation plan or limited in how the lesson might be delivered. T4c should be flexible enough to allow teachers to manipulate or change the delivery context as needed to benefit the class.

For instance, a class of strong individual self-learners might be able to handle an entire lesson plan on their own in a flipped-classroom delivery wherein each student is responsible for ingesting a lesson plan as homework. The teacher might decide to require written responses to a prompt or a test to assess their performance and execution of the requirements. For another class with less-strong learners, and a few key leaders, the teacher might have the students work in small groups with an assigned leader to manage the delivery and submission for the project.

CRITICAL THINKING

The critical thinking skills encompass the three advanced levels of Bloom's taxonomy: *analysis, evaluation,* and *creation*. A long-winded examination of critical thinking skills isn't warranted in this book as there have been volumes written about it in all disciplines from philosophy, education, business, and society in general. Relevant to this discussion is how technology can support and even enhance the development of critical thinking skills through leveraging the capabilities of technology systems, constructs, and simulations. Additionally, the way technology is leveraged to support collaboration allows all the models to be both synchronous and asynchronous, and most importantly, face-to-face or remote.

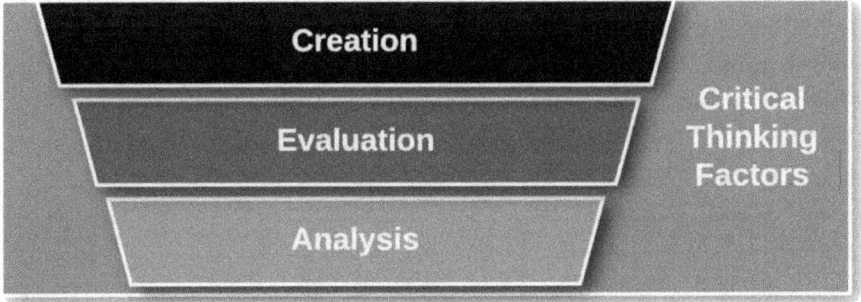

Figure 5.2. Critical Thinking Factors of Bloom's Taxonomy

Let's first look at how technology systems support the development and practicum of critical thinking on an individual basis, as the collaborative aspects are near infinite and warrant an in-depth but not an exhaustive analysis.

Analysis, Evaluation, and Creation

Technology systems can support and enhance analytical skills in the most fundamental ways as seen in the following examples, which are presented from the most rudimentary to the more complex.

As illustrated by these current day examples, cognitive factors in study and research are mastered and utilized to perform the advanced levels of the taxonomy, enhanced by technology systems available in most to all of today's educational environments, in particular:

- Computers on the Internet
- Office productivity suites
- Robotics and makerspaces
- 3-D printers
- Video cameras and video production software

Table 5.2. Individual Analysis, Evaluation, and Creation

Individual Analysis, Evaluation, and Creation Practicum
Reading a textbook online, then performing Internet-based research to understand more about the subject matter, as well as contradictory views
Reading a news article online and writing a "current events" analysis of the article
Viewing an animation video of an internal combustion engine and answer a prompt on a message board about how energy is conserved
Reading peer's comments on a message prompt and evaluating each response for validity and accuracy
Researching fossil fuels online by reading what their advocates and critics say to develop an independent opinion
Visiting an art gallery online and writing a paper on Impressionism
Studying HTML coding and writing simple scripts and functions
Writing a robotics program that allows a robot to navigate a map and pick up objects
Studying an automobile differential and creating it with a 3-D printer
Producing, directing, and broadcasting of a daily news and current events program for a school, district, or university

COLLABORATION

After reading the above examples of critical thinking skills and practicum leveraging basic technology systems, each example can be elevated to its collaborative evolution to impact small or large work groups, while also working on higher level interpersonal communication and organizational skills.

Table 5.3. Collaborative Practicum

Individual Analysis, Evaluation, and Creation Practicum	Collaborative Practicum
Reading a textbook online, then performing Internet-based research to understand more about the subject matter, as well as contradictory views	Then posting a report on the research and replying to comments from peers
Reading a news article online and writing a "current events" analysis of the article	Then using a shared document online to publish a daily online newspaper from multiple "reporters/journalists"
Viewing an animation video of an internal combustion engine and answering a prompt on a message board about how energy is conserved	Then working with a group of students to model how the individual systems of a car work together: fuel, engine, drivetrain, steering, brakes, etc.
Reading peer's comments on a message prompt and evaluating each response for validity and accuracy	Then each student must join a group to debate opposite positions of the prompt in an online video chat room
Researching fossil fuels online by reading what their advocates and critics say to develop an independent opinion	Then creating advocacy groups that organize committees to develop plans for legislative action
Visiting an art gallery online and writing a paper on Impressionism	Then using a shared painting program and forming small work groups to try to re-create specific artwork
Studying HTML coding and writing simple scripts and functions	Then assembling a group that writes an entire app for a mobile device with multiple objects
Writing a robotics program that allows a robot to navigate a map and pick up objects	Then entering the program in a competition with other teams to perform tasks competitively
Studying an automobile differential and creating it with a 3-D printer	Then having groups design and print various components of a car drivetrain from engine, transmission, drive shaft, differential, axles, and wheels
Producing, directing, and broadcasting of a daily news and current events program for a school, district, or university.	Then assigning each role to a group member and then rotating the responsibilities each week so each member experiences each role.

THE 6C SURVEY FORM FOR T4C DEVELOPMENT

Table 5.4. 6C Survey Form

Lesson Plan—Name		

Curriculum		Define the source of the curriculum content:
		    Where does it come from?
		    Is it current, relevant, and topical?

Core—Standards		Determine CCSS alignment:
		    Which standards does it align with?
		    What other standards can be synthesized?

Cognitive Factors		List the cognitive factors:
		    What are the factual items that are to be retained?
		    What cognitive factors are part of standard testing?

Context	Lesson Plan	Define the lesson scenario: What construct of behaviorism or realism can be employed to enhance the lesson content?

	Delivery	Define the delivery methodology:
		    How will the teacher deliver the content?
		    What technology systems will be employed?
		    How do the technology systems enhance the delivery?
		    What are the artifacts to be developed?

Critical Thinking		Define the practicum that will enforce critical thinking skills such as analyzing, evaluating, comparing, contrasting, and creating.
		    How will the LMS or other technology platforms support the practicum?
		    How does the practicum support the retention of the cognitive factors?

Collaboration		Define how students will collaborate (or not collaborate) for this lesson plan:
		    How will they be grouped?
		    What will be the leadership construct?
		    How will the technology system host and enhance the collaboration model?
		    How does the collaboration practicum enhance critical thinking?

ARTIFACTS—WHAT ARE THE RESULTANT T4C COMPONENTS?

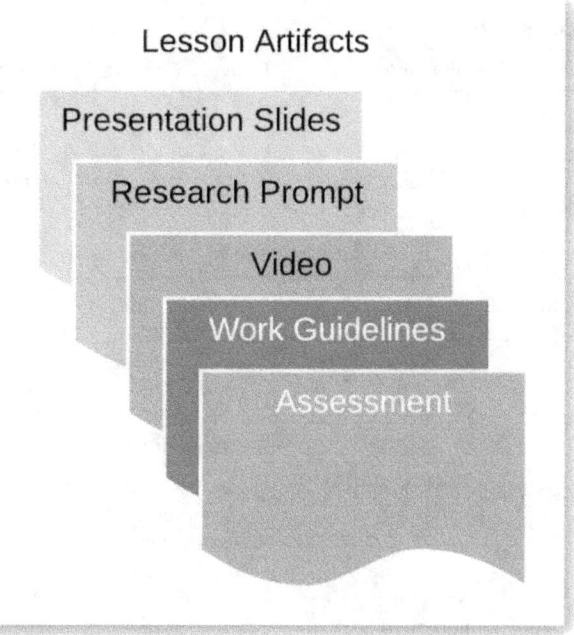

Figure 5.3. T4c Artifacts

The process should define the artifacts that encompass the T4c delivery and implementation. Luckily, the fourth C, Context, helps define what the artifacts might be. Further, the fifth and sixth Cs may also define platforms that support the practicum for critical thinking and collaboration.

Considering the example from the "Context" section of this chapter, the reader can see the delivery context provides much of the basis for determining the artifacts that will combine to create the T4c lesson.

Table 5.5. Example T4c Artifacts

Curriculum	Lesson Context	Delivery Context	Artifacts
All			6C Survey Form
Science/Biomes	Students are world explorers throughout various time periods	Using Google Maps and streaming videos to experience biomes	Slides Presentation Embedded or Linked Videos Web Survey Assessment
History/American Revolution	Students are colonialists and/or British politicians	News reporting crew as delivery using copy writing, layout, editing, publication	News Team Web Page GAFE Share Docs Video Production News Reel
English/Language Arts	Students describe elements of the story or skill focus (e.g., theme of a story) using interactive LMS like Prezi or PowToons, to display their understanding of the text	Students include examples of text evidence in presentation with visual animations, oral recordings, video recordings, text boxes, screenshots of the texts, pictures, etc.	MS PowerPoint Presentation Links or Embedded Video Web Pages
Math/Area	Students are architects	Using Google Draw to display square footage of a dream home they create. Group collaboration by having students create different features of home and aspects of creation	Computer Models Links or Embedded Video Formulas Animations Modeling (Live)

CHAPTER 5—ACTION ITEMS

1. *Develop Your School's 6C Survey Form:*
   Using the sample provided, develop your team's 6C Survey Form. Modify the questions in the survey as needed to derive the necessary information for your T4c development team.
   a. *Train a group of teachers in the process.*
      Unless you already have a T4c development team created, start by finding those "innovative teachers" scattered throughout the district and train them in the 6C development process. They'll also require some training on the LMS and development platforms and some basic standard for development.

      Consider starting a pilot program to provide time and incentive for these teachers to begin innovating for your school's T4c initiative.
2. *Develop a T4c Implementation Plan*
   Now that you have an organic T4c development effort started at the grass-roots level, develop a T4c Implementation Plan that will provide a road map for full-scale development and implementation.

CHAPTER 6

What's after the 6Cs?

What happens after the 6Cs are defined and developed? There are three more steps in the development lifecycle, but the name 6C—IAE just didn't sound right. These three additional steps are *implementation, assessment,* and *evaluation.*

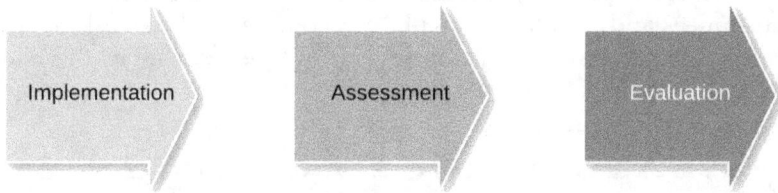

Figure 6.1. What's after the 6Cs?

IMPLEMENTATION

Implementation is, of course, delivering the lesson plan. Like any other lesson, the teacher—and the delivery of the lesson plan—make all the difference in the world. An enthusiastic teacher can be effective using the most rudimentary curriculum and tools, just recall some of your favorite grade-school teachers. Chances are their effectiveness had little to do with their curriculum and resources but rather with their energy and enthusiasm for the lesson and interest in their students.

Similarly, excellent curriculum and technology can be rendered ineffective in as many ways; for instance, a teacher's lack of interest and/or understanding of the curriculum as well as inefficient use of the technology, which can manifest itself in numerous ways. Maybe the Chromebooks weren't charged or the network was slow. Possibly there weren't enough devices for everyone, or many students weren't familiar with the interface. Whatever the impediment, the enthusiastic and able teacher will be able to deliver the lesson plan and objectives regardless.

Points for Solid Implementation

Points to help ensure solid implementation include the following:

ENSURE THE COGNITIVE FACTORS ARE OBVIOUS

It's not enough just to throw the names, dates, and locations to the students and hope for ingestion and regurgitation—that's what this whole book is about. The delivery of the lesson plan must accomplish all its explicit as well as implicit goals. It is incumbent of the teacher to provide the lesson and delivery context that makes names, dates, and locations come to life, to become a story within a scenario, a behaviorist reality that the student can experience and assimilate, to gain understanding into the circumstances and the environment, to become part of the lesson, and to become part of the world (of the lesson) but yet remember the names, dates, and locations at test time.

MAXIMIZE THE USE OF TECHNOLOGY IN THE DELIVERY CONTEXT

As stated earlier in this book, the lesson context is *partially* under the teacher's control, but the delivery context is *entirely* under the teacher's control. That means that the teacher is ultimately responsible for optimizing critical-thinking exercises and collaboration, all in the effort to help the student assimilate the lesson.

That also means that teachers need to have a deep understanding of all the technology tools available to the class and the students individually, and that the teacher is not just injecting technology-based activities that offer no additional benefit. For example, making students work in groups and then have a discussion on a message board is arguably redundant and non-beneficial. Now if the message board is used for peer review with students outside the work group, that would offer additional perspectives to the project.

Obviously, the computing platform and LMS (learning management system) must be available and functional, but if the teacher is not adept at all the collaborative capabilities of the LMS, they are missing out on the opportunity to empower their students with these features.

So, using message board peer review, functional work groups, and shared documents are surefire ways to enhance their understanding of the lesson and reinforce assimilation of the cognitive factors.

ASSESSMENT

As with any curricular instructional design, once the lesson plan is developed, it must have a performance assessment protocol as well as a curriculum assessment protocol. One is the student's, and the other is for the curriculum itself. How will the resultant curriculum be assessed for its effectiveness?

Student Assessment

For the student's assessment, define how students will be assessed as to their assimilation of the lesson plan:

How Will Their Understanding Be Demonstrated and/or Measured?

Will there be an individualized test or quiz? Will standard 0–10 scoring be used to keep things relative to other lesson assessments? As students move up in grade level and writing acumen, it becomes more relevant to use qualitative forms of assessment such as essay questions, long-form written analysis, and collaborative group responses. In addition, more experiential and behaviorist methods might be used for assessments as in the following:

- Write a news article about the lesson plan as a current event
- Compare and contrast possible outcomes from tests or experiments
- Analyze various geographical or regional variances to the lesson plan

How Will Their Results Determine If the Curriculum and Lesson Plan Is Effective?

Obviously, the primary indicator for lesson plan effectiveness would be gross test scores. However, it's clearly possible that the lesson plan assessment does not provide a valid indicator of the lesson's effectiveness. It's possible that the questions asked in a test or quiz only measure the cognitive factors of the lesson but don't provide the practical or functional comprehension required for analysis or comparison.

How Will Individual Student's Results Be Measured against Others?

This becomes another important factor for both the student assessment as well as the curriculum assessment. Is the lesson plan effective in the major aspects of the curriculum as to provide a level playing field for all the students? For instance, does a lesson plan based on a sports scenario favor students that practice in the sport or interest.

An example of this would be using a baseball team's batting statistics as a lesson for statistical analysis. Players of the sport might inherently have a deeper understanding of the application of the statistic and therefore score higher in the assessment.

How Will Overall Class Results Be Reported within the Course Plan?

Once this data is accumulated for the class, what are the relevant aspects of their collective success/failure in the student assessment? And how do these results impact the curriculum assessment. For example, if many students seem to score low on the lesson plan quiz, how should that affect the 6C factors? Particularly the lesson context and/or the delivery context.

Low scores in the assessment of cognitive factors might mean that the delivery context does not highlight the factors enough. While low analytical scores (reflecting lack of comprehension) might mean that the lesson context is not strong enough or not relevant to the student's learning perspective.

And Ultimately, What Were Their Test Results?

Just like any lesson assessment, do high test results mean true comprehension and assimilation, or that the assessment is too easy? All students scoring in the highest percentile might indicate the latter, while a variance of results, mostly high, might indicate the former. As well, the teacher can assess the cognitive factors or metrics of critical thinking and collaboration.

How Well Did They Analyze, Determine, or Compare/Contrast Factors of the Lesson Plan?

Obviously, factors of higher-grade levels and subjects must be taken into consideration, but students' ability to analyze, determine, and compare provide a significant window into their comprehension of the lesson plan. In this way, the teacher can then "fine tune" the delivery context of a lesson to best address the needs of the individuals in the class, as well as the classroom as a whole.

For instance, a teacher might have a Tier 4 curriculum (T4c) that requires some individuals to work singly while others work in a group. The flexibility of T4c based on the technology use model would allow lesson plans to be delivered in various focused delivery contexts based on the capabilities of the individuals and the individuals in work groups.

Did Their "Creation" Involve Creativity and Advanced Logic/Thought?

At the highest level of Bloom's taxonomy, creation demonstrates the student's ability to truly originate concepts and ideas reflective of the curriculum and lesson plan. This could be as simple as developing their own experiments that demonstrate relevant scientific experimentation or writing analysis of historical events through the development of a script or screenplay for a language arts or history class. Ask the question, is this creation reflective of data or comprehension gained through the lesson plan?

An example of this might be in a newspaper production scenario lesson context to which their assignment might be to cover the school's Veteran's Day Fair. The delivery context would be to have the news production team assign photographers and reporters to the event. These team members would work the event as individuals and deliver their content (photos and article) to the production team and editors. The production team would be three to four students in charge of graphic design, layout, and publication. The editorial board would be a group of students in charge of reviewing and approving the final edition for print.

In this scenario, the whole class works as a group, but some assignments are individuals doing work within a scope while others are working on the total deliverable product.

Will Additional Grade Consideration Be Applied for Leadership Roles?

This concept is obviously more geared toward work groups and collaboration. The delivery context of the lesson might dictate that the group select a leader—explicitly determined—and then the lesson plan might call for a separate grading rubric for the leaders of each group.

Will Additional Grade Consideration Be Applied for Performance Roles or Special Contributions?

This becomes one of the areas where the teacher can change or modify the assessment for each delivery of the lesson plan. Where group work or collaboration is a feature of the delivery context, students might take on various roles within the group, such as leader, spokesman, researcher and/or copywriter. The teacher can determine at the beginning of the lesson whether grades might be weighted differently based on the student's role within a collaboration.

Will Grades Be Balanced between the Work Group or Weighted by Some Process?

Again, this assessment might be weighted between the students differently based on the delivery context. A group leader might influence a larger percentage of the project and therefore might be entitled to more gross points. We'll include an assessment template at the end of this chapter. In terms of assessing the curriculum as developed, the teacher should assess if the curriculum and the 6C factors fulfill the curriculum objectives?

Did the Lesson Plan Reference/Leverage Existing Curriculum?

Although this is not necessarily an important 6C development factor, it does call into question whether the teacher is truly leveraging and adhering to the lesson cognitive factors and state standards. The last thing the district wants is a bunch of T4c developers straying away from the actual adopted curriculum and missing major points required to achieve standard testing requirements. Don't reinvent the wheel unless absolutely necessary, and stick to the testing standards.

Did the Lesson Plan Effectively Align with CCSS?

Once again, since achievement in standardized testing is a key success factor, this is an important criterion. But this question can only be answered through an assessment or testing. That means in order to prepare for standardized testing, the fundamental concepts and standards alignment become the evaluation criteria.

Did the Lesson Plan Effectively Communicate the Cognitive Factors?

The effectiveness of the delivery to communicate the cognitive factors becomes the salient part of the whole effort. What good is all this modeling and context if the students don't achieve the standards? Instructional designers and teachers should devote their time and efforts in defining delivery contexts that don't get caught up in the complexities of the scenarios and lose the effective communication of the cognitive factors.

One example of this was much more common when laptops and tablets were first introduced into classrooms. Teachers and students might spend their time dealing with the distribution of the technology, poor wireless connectivity, and lack of curriculum developed specifically for that delivery method. In the chaos of getting kids access to devices, the lessons and standards become lost in the fog of technology failure.

Was the Lesson Context Effective for That Lesson/Class/Student(s) Combination?

This assessment has to do with the lesson context and its effectiveness within the constraints of the students in the class. Clearly lessons for a remedial math class will require a varied context than might be presented to a class of high achievers.

For instance, students in a remedial English language arts (ELA) class might benefit from a very straight forward leader-led lecture and discussion of the subject matter. While an advanced placement (AP) ELA teacher might present a lesson to this class under a completely behaviorist scenario, engendering more critical thinking and collaborative opportunities for the student—same curriculum, different lesson context.

Did the Delivery Context Leverage Technology Systems to Enhance Delivery and Assimilation?

When assessing delivery context, the teacher must take into consideration the technology systems, and their accessibility to all the students, and how the delivery technology enhances the lesson context. What does that mean? Do the technology tools and applications support and/or enhance the lesson plan?

Here's an example of technology "substitution" where this is not the case: replacing the $100 overhead project and transparencies with ceiling-mounted projectors and screens at a hundred times the cost, only to have the teacher put their documents under the document camera. This is a powerful example of substitution not providing a clear return on investment.

The fullest evolution (T4c) of this example is where the teacher incorporates video, 3-D modeling, and tablet-based simulators to deliver a lesson plan that includes critical-thinking exercises.

Did the Lesson Plan Objective Require Analysis, Synthesis, and/or Critical Thinking?

This assessment gets to the point of critical thinking. Did the lesson plan *objective* require the key factors, or was the objective simply to ingest and regurgitate factoids? If the cognitive factors are simply names and dates in a history lesson plan, it will be upon the teacher to help assimilate the information through a lesson context that enhances and reinforces the information.

For example, in a historical lesson plan on the assassination of Lincoln, instead of listing all the parties present, a lesson context that has students assign characters and roleplay the final hours would help reinforce cognitive factors like the character names and locations, such as Ford's Theater and Henry Rathbone.

Did the Lesson Plan Effectively Utilize Technology to Facilitate Collaboration?

This is an area easy to synthesize into a delivery context. Having a peer review message interaction following a homework assignment allows students to reinforce cognitive factors by checking the work of other students. It also can enhance critical thinking through their analysis and critique of other students' participation in group work or projects.

EVALUATION

Evaluation of the T4c

Evaluation of the T4c is the stage where the teacher determines if the lesson plan is successful and a candidate for district standard curriculum. Some of the questions to be asked follow.

Are the Cognitive Factors Recognized?

Do the students retain the cognitive factors better through the T4c delivery? Do they recall them during standardized testing? If the answers to these questions are "yes," then mission accomplished.

Is the Lesson Context Well Accepted?

Does the experiential scenario help in conceptual and functional understanding of the curriculum? In other words, does the lesson context help or hinder the learning process?

For example, in the science/biomes example, does the "students are world explorers" help the students understand the varieties and differentiation of the biomes. Is their critical understanding of the biomes and how they affect human world explorers helpful in their assimilation of the scenario? Again, if the answers are "yes," then the lesson scenario is helpful and should be considered a successful lesson context for use in future implementations.

Is the Delivery Methodology Functional?

Did the delivery context enhance student critical thinking and lesson assimilation? Stated differently, do the technology and tools get in the way of the learning process?

If the LMS is not easy to understand and use, it might cause students to miss assignments or submit homework in the wrong folder. If there are not enough Chromebooks in the classroom for all the students, one or more students might fall behind or miss out on the interactive simulations.

IS THE CRITICAL THINKING PRACTICUM EFFECTIVE?

Critical thinking requires an intimate understanding of the subject matter and how it's relevant to the circumstances, history, cause and effect, and so on. Critical thinking practicum should increase fundamental understanding of the lesson and its cognitive factors, not the other way around. The cognitive factors cannot trigger or enhance understanding without context.

Evaluate the lesson and implementation for this leveraged impact. You could almost use a financial "return on investment" style review. Was the cost (effort) of implementing the practicum worth the resultant outcome (test scores)?

For example, if the delivery context included students creating web pages about their subject matter, but the web-page software was not intuitive, this could result in confusion and chaos and many students being unable to complete the assignment on time. This is a clear example of technology and its use becoming an impediment to learning and understanding. This evaluation may be easy and obvious, but it also might not be.

What if the web-page software was intuitive for native English speakers but difficult for ESL students? This impact might not be so obvious until several implementations of the delivery context where results start to bear this symptom.

DOES THE COLLABORATION PRACTICUM ENHANCE UNDERSTANDING, ASSIMILATION, AND ACHIEVE LESSON PLAN OBJECTIVES?

Similarly, again with the collaboration practicum. Did the exercise enhance critical thinking and ultimately understanding, resulting in elevated test scores?

It's certainly conceivable that one or all work groups might get tangled in technology issues, or even social interaction issues that impede learning and assimilation in a collaboration exercise. One example of this might be a Facebook-style social media platform, such as Edmodo, being used in the classroom. If the students are able and allowed to get off task, and the resulting "collaboration" is not beneficial to the lesson plan, then the collaboration practicum becomes an impediment. Use the return-on-investment (ROI) analysis method to measure the effect of collaboration.

We have not seen a peer review message board exercise become ineffective or invaluable when the teacher moderates the board closely. We have witnessed plagiarism, bullying, and coercion appear on nonmoderated boards. The teacher is always the key.

Evaluation Template

Use Table 6.1 to compile your assessment, implementation notes, and evaluation of a given lesson plan after delivery. The exercise of completing the table will trigger assessment and evaluation just in the endeavor. The ROI analysis is performed in the process of answering the prompt questions.

Now the entire T4c development process has been detailed, now what? Let's repeat the questions about *who*, *what*, and *when*? Why tackle these questions again? Because the first time these questions were raised, no answers were provided. Now that *how* (how to develop T4c) has been illustrated, let's go back and address *who*, *what*, and *when* (*where* and *why* are givens).

DESIGN VERSUS DEVELOPMENT

This is a rhetorical question that doesn't have to be answered because it will work itself out on its own. Because of the natural and intrinsic constraints within the educational organization/bureaucracy, it isn't as simple as "do as I ask" and "as you wish."

Even something as simple as doing a pilot project with a group of teachers requires board approval, or at least site-based administrative approval—pilot projects almost always mark the end of innovation.

It was stated earlier that standards are required, likely at the district and possibly the site level as well. The district may want standards for platforms, templates, logos, mascots, nomenclature, directories and contact information, and acceptable use. Sites may want standards for backgrounds and slide masters, mottos, and a slew of other things you haven't even thought of yet.

These things must be designed—but by whom? This is especially true when in the pilot phase. Leave it up to that innovative teacher that is doing the pilot to figure many of these things out on their own, but also leave it to a team of administrators to decide that someone else needs to take on these responsibilities and that innovative teacher can go back to their class.

Development occurs when all these standards are defined, pilot projects are successful, resources are identified and trained and then let loose to develop away for a year or so. That's when serious T4c starts coming out. So, now ask *who*, *what*, and *when*?

Table 6.1. T4c Evaluation Template

After 6C—Implementation, Assessment, and Evaluation—Lesson Plan—Name

Implementation	Ensure the cognitive factors are obvious.
	Maximize the use of technology in the delivery context.
	Ensure the students understand the requirements of the project requirements.
	Note difficulties in the lesson context and delivery context for the evaluation process.
Assessment Student Assessment	How will their understanding be demonstrated/measured?
	How will their results determine if the curriculum and lesson plan is effective?
	How will individual student's results be measured against others?
	How will overall class results be reported within the course plan?
	What were their test results?
	Did the lesson plan reference/leverage existing curriculum?
	Did the lesson plan effectively align with CCSS?
	Did the lesson plan effectively communicate the cognitive factors?
	Was the lesson context effective for that lesson/class/student(s) combination?
	Did the delivery context leverage technology systems to enhance delivery and assimilation?
	Did the lesson plan objective require analysis, synthesis, and/or critical thinking?
	Did the lesson plan effectively utilize technology to facilitate collaboration?
Assessment Critical Thinking and Collaboration Assessment	How well did they analyze, determine, or compare/contrast factors of the lesson plan?
	Did their "creation" involve creativity and advanced logic/thought?
	Will additional grade consideration be applied for leadership roles?
	Will additional grade consideration be applied for performance roles or special contributions?
	Will grades be balanced between the work group or weighted by some process?
Assessment 6C Factors	Did the lesson plan reference/leverage existing curriculum?
	Did the lesson plan effectively align with CCSS?
	Did the lesson plan effectively communicate the cognitive factors?
	Was the lesson context effective for that lesson/class/student(s) combination?
	Did the delivery context leverage technology systems to enhance delivery and assimilation?
	Did the lesson plan objective require analysis, synthesis, and/critical thinking?
	Did the lesson plan effectively utilize technology to facilitate collaboration?
Evaluation	Are the cognitive factors recognized?
	Is the lesson context well accepted?
	Is the delivery methodology functional?
	Is the critical thinking practicum effective?
	Does the collaboration practicum enhance understanding, assimilation, and achieve lesson plan objectives?

WHO

Just go through the list of resources who could be fully or partially engaged in T4c development in Table 6.2.

WHAT

That wasn't so bad. The plan identified various resources in most school districts whom could be a T4c developer. From this analysis it can be seen that when a teacher is a developer, they are more likely to be a subject matter expert (SME) and not a true instructional designer. A district designated designer/developer would bring true standardization to a district-wide T4c development effort.

A hybrid of this example would be to have district-based developers/designers and site-based SMEs developing T4c in collaboration. The district resources then become the enforcers and design/development resources to the various site and grade-level teacher/SMEs.

To expand on the site-based grade-level development model, a grade-level development team might act as an SME team for a curriculum and then submit their materials and curriculum to the district team for compliance and approvals.

Development of T4c can take on a formal or an informal process. Just by training designated district resources, they could become designees or central-points-of-contact for advanced curriculum development. With basic guidance and leadership within the instructional services the T4c team could have an assortment of smaller artifact development projects and larger full-curriculum programs such as broadcast video productions, mock trials, robot competitions, or election debates.

WHEN

Now—if not now, next semester, or next year. But now that the plan has been laid out, what could you possibly be waiting for? Since nothing in a school district happens overnight, these types of initiatives may take months or, more likely, years to plan, justify, and execute. And since the discussion is about organizational structures, FTE resources, and funding, this discussion is really reserved for district instructional leadership.

But that doesn't mean that these concepts and models can't be advocated for and developed organically at the site-level, that may be a pilot or proof-of-concept phase. Once teachers and leadership see the results

Table 6.2. Who Will Develop Tier 4 Curriculum

Who Will Develop the T4c?

Teachers	Teachers are the ultimate SMEs for their curriculum and development because the best T4c has the delivery context in mind, and the teacher being the developer implicitly understands the proposed delivery context. The main caveat to having teachers be curriculum developers becomes these questions:
	     When will they do this development?
	     What standards for T4c do they adhere to?
	 The biggest risk is the development of a whole discipline of T4c that is so specific that it can't be shared site wide or district wide. Although this can help proliferate T4c within the district, there should be an approval process to ensure that there are standards for look-and-feel, navigation, and attribution.

Site Resource or TOSA	Having a resource focused on T4c at the site level might be hard to justify in any particular school or district. It is probably more likely to have a teacher with open periods who could be designated as a T4c development resource for the site. Maybe each site could have a collection of teachers designated for this type of development role—once again, how these resources are justified is not addressed in this discussion. This would ensure that development would adhere and/or comply with site-wide and/or district-based standards for T4c development. This resource might even be a developer of these standards. It also becomes clear that if there is a site-based resource or assigned teacher, there would need to be a district-based resource to organize and facilitate their collective efforts, otherwise a similar type of unique development effort might come from each site with no, or limited, adherence to standards.
District Resource or TOSA	Having a resource focused on T4c at the district level is much more viable as this is a typical resource in the instructional services department. Districts may also have media technicians or other media staff (think librarians) who could be designated for this role.

District FTE	In a larger district able to dedicate funds and headcount to this type of instructional development resource, an instructional designer might be hired specifically for the initial design and development of the district standards for T4c development. Once these standards are developed and approved, then this resource could begin the daunting task of a full-scale T4c development effort.
	 This district-centralized resource could lead the development of district-based standards for T4c development. This district-based resource would also become the obvious designee for the following types of development and organizational tasks:
	     District representative to county or state consortiums of curriculum development
	     District designated resource for all digital learning resources, such as:
	         Streaming video resources
	         Digital content libraries
	         T4c development communities
	         T4c training support resources.
	 In this case, this type of dedicated design/development resource would likely *not* be an SME for any particular subject or discipline. They would be an SME for the development platforms and standards themselves.

of such development efforts, more funding, training, and resources must be committed.

This comes back to strategic planning at the superintendent and assistant superintendent levels of any school or district. It's obvious why this whole "moving up the spectrum" ultimately takes multiple years, and why the need to jump straight to the top!

CHAPTER 6—ACTION ITEMS

1. *Develop a T4c Evaluation Template*

   Have your T4c pilot team use the 6C Evaluation Template provided to customize your school's own Evaluation Template based on the requirements of your initiative and the type of T4c under development.

2. *Develop a T4c Development Team Structure and Implementation Plan*

   Begin to define what your school's T4c development team will look like. How many resources? How many program managers, instructional designers, and SMEs?

   a. *Who*

   Begin to identify actual staff and resources identified to be potential candidates for the T4c development team.

   b. *What*

   Begin planning how each individual staff member might be moved from their current position to a T4c designated team member. Will it be a lateral move? Will job positions need to be created and interviews conducted?

   What is the departmental budget impact?

   c. *When*

   When is the target date for start of operations? How long to develop standards for T4c development?

   d. *Where*

   Begin planning for where these staff and resources will be placed. Will they be district- or site-based?

   How will they communicate and report to the T4c development team program manager?

Chapter 7

Disrupting Incremental Innovation

ADVOCACY

So, let's talk a little about advocacy. Earlier chapters discussed how sanction and endorsement must come from the highest levels. Nothing could be better than the superintendent and instructional assistant superintendent to be an advocate of Tier 4 curriculum (T4c) development and support the initiative with district- and site-based infrastructure, resources, platforms, standards, and professional development. But don't expect them to "get it" all right now, simultaneously.

Organic growth of a T4c initiative could and will sprout out of the classroom. There's always that one, or group, of innovative teachers that takes the next step, commits their own time and resources, and engages with their students in developing curriculum that has all the elements of T4c. The limiting factor for these projects is always vision.

Although the teacher(s) have the vision of their media-rich, interactive lessons, they are usually centered around a subject matter or discipline. Usually gaining notoriety at the site- or district-level as a highlighted success, and then left to grow or die on its own. Without recognition of the innovations that make any new curriculum successful, there is no end reward for all the extra effort undertaken.

What happens when this group of innovative teachers are split up and/or moved to new classes, grade levels, and schools? Of course, these pockets of innovation dry up, and at best, the curriculum is used for several years by several teachers.

Someone has to gather these highlighted successes, pilot projects, and curriculum innovations and do something with them. Something that can ultimately provide the basis for a district-wide initiative for advanced curriculum. So, who is that someone?

ORGANIC GROWTH

So how to take that now-forsaken pilot project and turn it into organic growth that then takes root and grows into site- and district-wide adoption? Recognition that a full-scale curriculum development team might be warranted.

The question is how to take these innovation successes and use them to foster the expansion in development of T4c for the benefit of the whole school/district. The answer? The *champion*.

Every school needs a champion. The champion may be a teacher or administrator, but the champion must become the advocate for T4c and take it to the highest level. Of course, the higher level within the district organization that the champion holds, the better positioned he or she will be to make a truly consequential effort to create a district-wide T4c initiative.

To start, let's take the example of that "innovative" teacher being discussed. There are usually many, and they are scattered throughout the district. The trick is to get their "pilot project" out of the barn and introduced to the masses. The innovation must be positioned, not as a pilot for a single discipline or grade level, but as a groundswell for a new advanced curriculum and a method for rapid development and deployment.

These innovative teachers may lose their enthusiasm and stop innovating. The school must identify these innovations as opportunities to induce, inspire, and promote the recognized need for technologically enabled curriculum. If the first problem is still in educating the masses about SAMR (substitution, augmentation, modification, and redefinition), then the new age challenge is to introduce the concept of developing at the highest level of SAMR—or Tier 4.

But by whatever name the initiative may take, the vision must be to introduce a model that scales to the "Nth" degree, to encompass and enable the district as a whole. And just to reinforce the point, it's not about having static curriculum, it's about the capacity and ability to continue to develop this level of curriculum and to stay at the top of the innovation curve.

PILOT PROJECTS

So now the pilot project takes on a whole new meaning under the umbrella of T4c. The effort isn't to develop a single lesson plan that fully engages the students of one classroom, but to develop a model that empowers teachers and site- and district-based resources to develop T4c and put them into district-wide distribution within a one- to two-year time frame. This way the resultant T4c lessons can have immediate impact on students and standardized testing and then become the basis for incremental new development over succeeding years.

The champion and the innovative teachers within the pilot project must focus their efforts on building out the T4c production line. Think of Henry Ford. Although typically credited as inventor of the automobile, historians understand that his most significant innovation was the production line and the concept of mass production.

Mass production of automobiles in the early twentieth century is the perfect example of the environment today with the SAMR model and education technology. The innovation of the production line is the perfect example of how to disrupt the slow progression and adoption of technologically enabled curriculum and jump to the top of the model. *It's not about the technology!* It's about what the technology enables. The 6Cs.

At the beginning of the automobile mass production process, there was the carriage (think horse-drawn), then the motor, then the drivetrain, and so on. Once the initial automobile was designed, then mass production processes needed to be developed to keep up with demand. They needed a "production line" to streamline the production of the chassis, engines, transmissions, and drivetrains. This need fostered a whole new line of innovations related to mass production of automobiles. Automobile manufacturing went from ten cars per day to Ford's Model T of which as many as ten thousand could be built in a day!

In a pure T4c scenario, first a school needs infrastructure. It's literally taken almost forty years to promulgate and deploy adequate infrastructure into schools in order to make the move to T4c possible. Just as cars could only drive on paved roads (as opposed to horse and stagecoach trails), T4c can only be delivered in a fully ubiquitous technology infrastructure, from cabling up through student devices and cloud applications—*2020 is truly the year for T4c!*

So, the champion must no longer focus on curriculum. He or she must turn the focus on the infrastructure, platforms, processes, and professional development necessary to design and implement a "production line" for T4c. If this effort can be adopted and resourced at the district level, it has the best chance and opportunity for success.

CLEARINGHOUSE

Once this first step is underway, and a T4c development group has been created and sanctioned, the next step will be to store and catalog their curriculum. What could be more impactful for early development than immediate adoption and implementation of the curriculum? That means it must be available, easy to identify, easy to implement, and available to all teachers. Think about a district's private YouTube catalog of T4c ready and available for any and all teachers to put into immediate use in their classrooms.

If the resultant T4c lesson plans achieve all the objectives of the 6C development process, then teachers throughout the district—or even state—could begin to implement, evaluate, and adopt the new curriculum as they are introduced. By year two, there's no reason why all newly developed T4c shouldn't be in mass implementation.

SITE-WIDE INITIATIVES

At the site level, a principal as champion is in the position to define and organize a T4c development team made up of several technology-adept teachers and possibly a teacher on special assignment (TOSA) who can dedicate their time to defining and developing this production line. Once the production process is defined and implemented, it can be introduced and implemented at each site, nurturing site-wide initiatives. Again, the focus of the development group is to model the production of T4c and then begin production.

GRADE-LEVEL INITIATIVES

Another opportunity to grow a T4c development initiative organically would be as a grade-level initiative, taking a site or district grade-level committee, training them in T4c development, and have them convert the curriculum over a period of one to two years. Once the process is developed within the district, the process can be rolled out at all grade levels or other grade levels.

DISTRICT-WIDE INITIATIVES

A district-wide, but organically grown initiative might start as a pilot project within education services. If a champion emerged out of the ed services group with the T4c development concept, they could launch a pilot across sites, likely as a grade-level curriculum upgrade project.

This team would be uniquely positioned to create the curriculum in collaboration with grade-level SMEs (subject matter experts) across sites, and also would have access to the infrastructure to warehouse and become the centralized clearinghouse for T4c curriculum. This is probably the scenario for organically grown T4c most likely to press beyond pilot project (purgatory) onto a full-blown district-wide initiative.

STATE-WIDE INITIATIVES

This of course would be the be-all, end-all best scenario of a full-scale T4c initiative. California tends to be too big to operate state-wide initiatives, but there is no reason that smaller states with stronger, more influential state education departments couldn't embark on a T4c initiative. Just get this book in front of the right politicians!

STRATEGIES FOR IMPLEMENTATION AND DEPLOYMENT —CREATING A T4C DEVELOPMENT TEAM

Who Are They and Where Did They Come From?

Only at the district level can a fully implemented T4c development process become an ongoing district entity. Its objective need not be specific, meaning there doesn't need to be a designated "T4c Development Team" as much as there needs to be T4c developmentally trained resources. Any teacher or resource should be able to develop curriculum following the T4c guidelines and structure. With applicable standards, practices, templates, and support resources, a district can get into the T4c development business and support and maintain the capability in-house in perpetuity.

Once the standards, processes, and procedures are developed and the instructional resource staff has been trained, then the district can be at true T4c district. This is not just a district with resources designated for T4c development but all development resources adhere to the standards and guidelines for that districts' curriculum and all resources (not just teachers) can be an SME and a T4c developer.

If the reader could envision how the ideal T4c development team would be organized, trained, and provided with all the necessary development resources and time, what would that team look like? What training would they require? What resources would they need? A more strategic approach would be to ask the following questions.

WHAT IS THE MISSION OF THE T4C TEAM?

Just as in any strategic planning exercise, the overriding mission should be defined in the earliest stage of planning. This mission must be driven by a *vision*. Does this discussion sound familiar?

By using a structured approach to planning, the task is less daunting. In this case it's good to be discussing an area more granularly specific than "Why T4c?" At this point of the discussion, the objective is defining a mission for a T4c development team.

Who Defines This Mission?

It's safe from an author's perch to propose that the cabinet would define the mission. And it might be as simple as "staff and implement a T4c development team that will define platforms and standards and develop T4c for district-wide use."

Who Will Lead the Team?

It's impossible to propose how the leader of this team is identified, recruited, and/or deployed within your organization, but it can be envisioned by defining job tasks and activities this team leader will perform. Organize and manage a team of resources, including the following:

- Instructional Designers—designer/developer of actual curriculum/lesson plan components. Experts at standards and platform implementation; supports clearinghouse and archive of curriculum.
- SMEs—teachers and other instructional resources providing subject-matter and/or discipline specific resources, content and/or curriculum.
- Graphic Designers—teachers and other instructional resources skilled at creating graphic images and designs to enhance T4c. Graphic designers would be resources for curriculum development as well as for specific lesson plan components such as diagrams, flowcharts, graphs and blueprints, and other lesson enhancing imagery. They may also develop animations and simple video clips.
- Video Production Technician—staff/resources dedicated to custom development of video products, such as documentary video, video projection, and video editing.
- Project Managers—resources/staff dedicated to organizing staff, coordinating resources and schedules to support project and curriculum development milestones

Your district's team may have more or less of these members, but the skill sets will be required for full-fledged T4c development.

WHAT ARE THE QUALIFICATIONS AND EXPERIENCE NECESSARY TO BE ON THE T4C DEVELOPMENT TEAM?

Requisite Skills for The Team Leader

Deep Understanding of SAMR and T4c Concept

This may be too much to ask for unless you make reading this book a prerequisite for taking on the T4c team leader position. This sounds like a "catch-22," so let's just say, if you're inclined to formalize a department dedicated to technology-enabled curriculum, then make this book required reading.

Unfortunately, just understanding SAMR alone will not suffice. With all the writings available about SAMR, there still hasn't been any specific roadmap to developing curriculum at the redefinition level (Tier 4) of the model. In fact, most of the writing about SAMR simply defines the model and provides a light dusting on the descriptions of each level and guidance for progressing up the levels.

Experience with LMS Platforms, Presentation, and Productivity Applications

Any teacher that has recently completed any college-level online course will likely have significant exposure to learning management systems (LMS) such as Blackboard, Moodle, or Google Classroom. The good news is that college-level online courses are mostly T4c compliant.

The primary distinguishing fact between T4c and the current college-level online course is that the T4c lesson plan would be developed using the 6Cs development process, which ensures that resultant curricula and lesson plans provide all the necessary components of true T4c as defined in this book.

The MS Office Suite (or Google Apps for Education) are the key building blocks of basic T4c lesson plans. Ninety percent of most T4c lesson plan components can be developed and delivered using the basic LMS and Office (or Google) Productivity Suites.

More sophisticated lesson plan components, such as animations, video clips, and/or interactive web pages require additional skills beyond LMS and productivity. Obviously, synchronous interactivity with peers or groups requires video conferencing capabilities and the flexibility in the delivery again is entirely under the teacher's control.

Basic Web-Page Development

Basic web-page development can add significant value to delivery context by enabling individual teachers to use tools like MS Publisher or

WordPress to publish web pages in support of their class resources, rendering them immediately available to students via web browser.

Instead of files within folders to be downloaded and completed, web pages can add rich media and integrate electronic and streaming resources to the students in an interactive mode. Web pages can be much more compelling and engaging because of the ability to create buttons, embed video/audio clips, and truly interact with the student as opposed to the student downloading and uploading files via Explorer.

Although requiring more development time from the teacher (initially), if the teacher's routine would be to develop and update the web pages exclusively as the session progresses, a complete chronology of that session and delivery context would now be in published web pages and could then be modified and updated each succeeding session.

This concept would require the teacher developing their T4c straight to web pages via the publishing platform instead of using Slides or PowerPoint to develop presentation files, which could then be used for presentation or for distribution to students. The web pages could become the presentation platform allowing all the integration capabilities of presentation software with the web-published aspect. This does require the teacher to become more familiar with web-page development and publishing with HTML and other web-coding platforms.

Project Management

If you've read either of the author's project planning and project management books, you know that he believes that *everyone* is a project manager. Every project or task within the realm of education curriculum and development requires some degree of project management.

By using project management techniques for planning, scope definition, resource planning time and schedule management, and communications, teachers, administrators, and curriculum developers can be in constant communication to support each other in the T4c development process.

Organizational Reporting

As with any departmental resource that is out of the classroom, organizational reporting becomes part of the resource's deliverable. For a T4c development team, the team leader must be an expert at project planning and project management. This means that the team leader should be able to report the following:

- Monthly/weekly projects
- Project timelines and resource reports

- Curriculum delivery windows
- Professional development plans and schedules

Other Preferred Skills

VIDEO PRODUCTION

The ability to take raw video and utilize a video editing and production software such as Adobe Premier, Corel VideoStudio, Pinnacle Studio, and/or Apple iMovie can be the difference between boring slide presentations versus compelling video/audio produced and edited specifically to suit the lesson plan and delivery context. Just as a picture is worth a thousand words, video is worth a thousand pictures—literally.

Video/animation with engaging audio tracks either in the form of music or narration can bring raw video to life and create the most-true-to-life experiences for the students. Combine this ability to create customized video for curriculum with the ability to embed them into interactive web pages and online curriculum can become very experiential and engaging. When customized to create critical-thinking exercises and practicum, the video clips take static presentations to the next level.

GRAPHIC DESIGN AND LAYOUT

Teachers and T4c developers with a natural graphic design talent can easily become valuable resources for curriculum development. These skills allow a basic slide deck with outline format to come alive with color palettes and graphics to support the lesson plan. We're not just talking about adding a color template and stock graphic images to a simple presentation slide deck.

We're talking about the ability to create inviting and interesting slides and backgrounds that complement the standards and textual components of a lesson plan. By using clip art and stock images to enhance a bulleted view, the standard slide format can be made much more interesting.

Once again, however, these enhancements cannot be random. Just adding color and changing font types can have an equally negative affect on curriculum and lessons by rendering them incomprehensible or illegible. Think of a slide deck that looks more like a ransom note than a well-developed graphical scheme.

INSTRUCTIONAL DESIGN

What makes an instructional designer? A resource dedicated to the development of curriculum and lesson plans or a recent instructional design graduate that gets a job doing that. The point being is that in a T4c development team, the dedicated instructional designer becomes the "producer and director" of the curriculum leveraging SMEs for the content and learning context.

By dedicating these resources—as opposed to having a team of developers—this allows the instructional designers to be focused on the adherence to standards of design and navigation, documentation, and preparation, while the SMEs can focus entirely on content, research, and data integrity and attribution.

CODING AND WEB DEVELOPMENT

Any team resource that can code has a leg up on the customized webpages aspect of curriculum development. True interactive lessons where the students click and interact with interfaces can only be created using web development tools. This the difference between self-guided curriculum modules and productivity applications such as PowerPoint.

No matter how much development and customization, MS PowerPoint and Google Slides can only offer the capability for lecture-format, or teacher-delivered presentation. Even though both suites offer a "kiosk" mode that allows the presentation to run automatically and loop, the depth of user interaction is really a mouse click on an arrow or a < or > key press. Similarly, if the slide deck is output to a (Adobe PDF [.pdf]) format, the presentation can be locked and unchangeable, and readable without having MS PowerPoint available, but the level of "interactivity" is just mouse-clicking forward or reverse.

A web developer can create interactive pages with customized buttons, embedded video/audio, and program a high-level of interactivity into a single web page or a full-blown website. Beyond that, smartphone apps that run on Apple iPhone and Google Android operating systems can also be developed to enhance BYOD (bring your own device) environments.

What Would Be the Year-One Objectives?

This question really caps off the question of creating a T4c development team. What can they hope to accomplish in the first year? Let's put it this way, the more guidance and direction provided in the inception of the team, the faster they can get to work. Again, does that mean that they have to read this book? Unless you've found another book that details how to build this team and what they should be doing better than this one, I'd have to say YES!

If a district commits to creating a T4c development team, then they have already recognized the following requisite and prerequisite concepts:

1. There is a district defined T4c set of platforms and standards:
   a. LMS—Google Classroom
   b. Development platforms—GAFE, Adobe, Corel
   c. Development, backgrounds, and interface standards
2. T4c development team:
   a. Team leader/project manager
   b. Instructional designer(s)
   c. SMEs
3. Year-one objectives
   a. Identify T4c starting points
   b. Develop a design and development process 24-month plan
   c. GO LIVE!

WORK REQUEST PROCESS

Once the T4c team is operational, it is inevitable that certain instructional groups will have priority requests for T4c development. Like any information technology (IT) request, there should be a survey form that the requestors complete in order to provide the necessary information to the T4c development team.

Keep in mind, they don't need to create design specifications, they need to provide curriculum name, objective, and program constraints (scope, time, and budget) that will provide priority and timelines and any additional resources that might be necessary to formalize a project. The following workflow process is a sample of how any IT work request process might work. Feel free to adapt this workflow for your T4c work request process:

Work Request Process Flow

Project Initiation: The T4c development process should include a list or survey of eligible T4c requestors. These are the people who are designated to make requests for curriculum. It may be decided that requests come from individual teachers and/or department heads, or maybe the T4c team may determine that requests come through the principals. Whatever works, there needs to be a designated group approved and trained in the process, otherwise the T4c development team will be inundated with random and unsolicited and unvetted work requests.

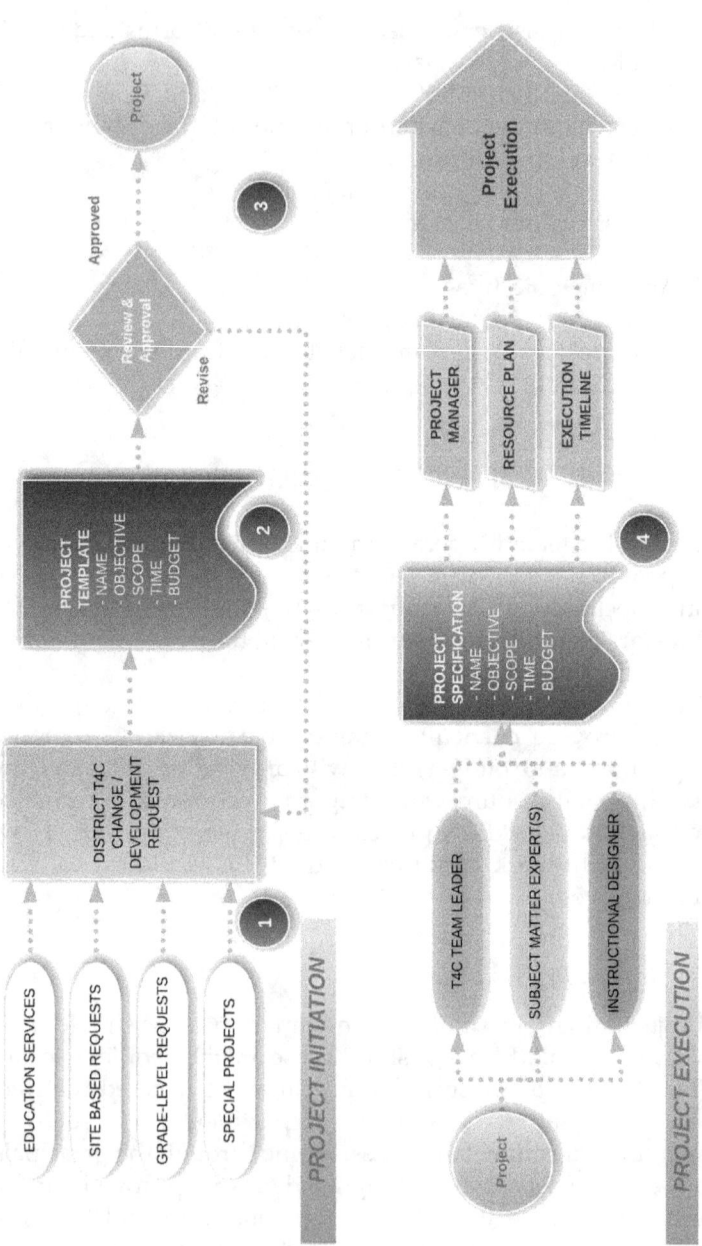

Figure 7.1. Tier 4 Curriculum Work Request Process

DESIGNATED REQUESTORS (1)

In this workflow example there are four groups defined to create T4c work requests:

- Education Services—the designee might be the assistant superintendent of education services and/or a designee from this group.
- Site-Based Requests—these might come from site department heads and/or the principals and his or her designees.
- Grade-Level Requests—if grade level committees exist across schools, they are a logical T4c work request group.
- Special Projects—special projects might be identified by cabinet or other designated instructional group or specific funding within the district.

1. District T4c Development/Change Request

    An electronic request form might be developed as a web-page form or even an MS Word template to identify the work request. The T4c work request would provide the following information.
    a. Project Template
    b. Project Name—The project name becomes the district identity of the project. It should define specifically what the T4c is and for whom it is developed; for example, third-grade science/biomes or twelfth-grade history American government—Constitution.
    c. Objective—The requestor's committed or interest group will define the objective for the T4c. This objective will provide the T4c development team's basis for the 6Cs process: Curriculum, Core, Cognitive Factors, Context, Critical Thinking, and Collaboration.

    It cannot be assumed that the requestors have been trained in the 6C definition process, but the T4c development team (instructional designers and SMEs) would be able to define and determine the 6Cs through their experience and conversations with the requestors.
    d. Scope—This can be the requestor's group or team. The scope will be defined by the audience, such as third graders or high school seniors.
    e. Time—This would provide a target completion date for the team. It might prove that the time requirement cannot be met.
    f. Budget—This would be a district internal transaction (or lack of transaction). In the world of school district interdepartmental billing/services, this could take on a variety of forms, but it must be defined if additional resources, external SMEs, or functional requirements are out of the typical develop scope and require additional funding or resources.

2. Approval Process

    The approval process ensures that each project is properly defined and vetted before commitment of resources and time. The T4c team leader is obliged to perform this vetting as due diligence to committing resources to a comprehensive approach to T4c development. We're not talking about building a slide deck. We're talking about engaging resources—project manager, instructional designer, and SMEs—and having this team perform the 6C assessment and definition process. This process will define the 6Cs, but it doesn't define each component of the lesson plan and the lesson context.

3. Assign Project Team

    Once the T4c project has been successfully vetted and approved by the T4c team leader, resources and designers/developers will be assigned. They will be provided with the project template, and identify the project manager, resource plan, and execution timeline.

What about execution you ask? Well that's a project, and if you need help with project planning and project management, the author's book *Project Management in the Ed Tech Era: How to Successfully Plan and Manage Your School's Next Innovation* (Vidal 2018) is the perfect text for that.

For this book, once the project team has been assigned, they are accountable to provide the lesson plan outline (based on the 6C survey form) and the curriculum artifacts to the district curriculum clearinghouse for use by all teachers.

CHAPTER 7—ACTION ITEMS

1. *Initiate a Pilot Project*

    Now is the time to initiate and start the pilot project that will kick-off your school's T4c development initiative. Remember that this pilot project must net results in the form of T4c products (lesson plans and artifacts) that can be stored in the clearinghouse and put into implementation by the teacher community.

    Don't let this pilot project languish in purgatory. Make sure it provides not only the T4c lessons but also the justification for the full-scale T4c development team.

    a. *Must Be Backed By Resources (Staff and Cloud Services)*

        The pilot project will be a scaled-down version of your T4c development team plan but don't use that as a reason not to put all available resources behind the effort.

Think program manager, instructional designer, SME. But also think about video production, graphic design, and web developer. The more resources detailed in your plan the greater objectives and goals that can be imagined.

If you tell your tech coordinator, "Okay, you are our T4c development team pilot project," you're not going to get the combined vision of a collaboration of those innovative teachers and a T4c champion with the scope to plan a formal pilot that leads up to a multiyear implementation plan.

2. *Plan Large-Scale Initiatives*
   a. *Site-based*

   A site-based pilot program might be to create a two- to three-person T4c development team at a secondary or K–8 site (where more advanced T4c can be modeled). Within this small group, each team member should fulfill multiple roles and skills, this team would have the advantage of a more cohesive group of SMEs and teachers for whom to develop T4c. A single teacher (SME) can work with the team to develop a complete T4c lesson (plan and artifacts) and begin to develop a library of content over time.

   Additionally, developing standards for content, user interface, navigation, and color palettes is one degree more granular, and less complex, than developing such standards at a district-wide level.

   b. *Grade-level*

   Another concept for a T4c pilot development team would be across a grade level. Assigning a T4c development team to develop a core curriculum for an entire grade-level would again provide a cohesive cohort for whom to develop T4c. For instance, developing the history, science, and ELA curriculum for the entire nineth-grade class would then allow a complete T4c library for that grade level and the associated teachers. In the second cycle, the team might advance to the next grade level along with the students and teachers.

   c. *District-wide*

   Obviously, the best pilot initiative would be at the district level. Especially at a large school district that would have the staff and resources to fully commit to a T4c development team with a fully staffed core team, tech experts (video, graphic, and web developer) and catalog of SMEs.

   This team would also need access to the best technology for all these platforms. The T4c that results should demonstrate the

highest level of all the aspects detailed in the 6C development process and professionally produced and tightly integrated into the district technology systems.
3. *Create a T4c Development Team*

    Okay, time to put up or stop talking about it. Lay the groundwork, convince the right people (leadership), find the talent (that innovative teacher or coordinator), give them this book, and say, "Get to work. What else do you need?"

Chapter 8

Full-Scale T4c Deployment

This book has now touched on every aspect of Tier 4 curriculum (T4c) development from vision, through definition (the 6Cs), to the development process. Then it detailed how to organize a T4c development team and what that team might look like—the required and preferred skill sets.

Now it's time to discuss some other critical success factors.

TECHNOLOGY SKILLS

The next critical success factor is regarding the user base—teachers. Teachers don't need to understand the whole 6C development process. That doesn't mean that every teacher must read this book, although the author would certainly like that. The next section of this chapter enumerates most of the requisite skills that teachers must possess in order to deliver T4c. Take a moment to review the 6C process. Reanalyze their relevance to the teacher experience, this time in the perspective of the teacher.

1. Curriculum

Not much to discuss in this aspect except that the teacher must have the relevant familiarity with the curriculum in order to deliver it and assess student performance. It would also make perfect sense that the teacher can review the 6C survey form, which should be one of the artifacts in the lesson plan to refamiliarize themselves with the curriculum.

2. Core

Similarly, teachers should be familiar with the state standards regarding their students, grade-level, and testing standards. By reviewing the 6C survey form, the teacher can reference the standards and can also determine if additional standards or relevant lessons can be added to the implementation of this lesson plan.

3. Cognitive Factors

By reviewing the cognitive factors for the lesson and how relevant they are to the standardized testing, the teacher is reminded to which cognitive factors to focus students' attention. Once again, the 6C survey form becomes a key for the teacher in any lesson plan implementation.

4. Context

(A) LESSON CONTEXT

The lesson context is mostly defined by the T4c as defined by the development team but that doesn't mean that the lesson context is inflexible. In fact, the teachers should use their discretion to enhance the lesson context via their own experiences and examples as applicable to their student base.

For instance, if the students are in a rural school, a historical lesson context based around an urban family and their struggles with discrimination might be revised to a more rural relatable lesson context of a farming family struggling with similar, or possibly even reverse discrimination. The lesson plan artifacts might not offer a similar level of flexibility.

(B) DELIVERY CONTEXT

As stated in earlier discussion about the delivery context, this tends to be the most customizable aspect of T4c and the area the teacher should seek to define and implement according to the students. In fact, it might be determined by the teacher that the same class section, taught in two different periods (with different students) might have a completely different delivery context.

Even though the T4c development team will have a proposed delivery context described in the 6C survey form, the teacher will have the ultimate discretion to customize the delivery. For instance, one class might be college-prep learning the same historical section as a remedial class. The college-prep students might be given more flexibility to work in collaborative work groups, or offered more advanced and flexible submission guidelines, while the remedial students would be required to adhere closely to the T4c artifacts and delivery context defined.

5. Critical Thinking

The 6C survey form will detail for the teacher the intended practicum (student exercises) that were intended to exercise critical thinking skills: analyzing, evaluating, comparing, contrasting, and creating. Based on the artifacts and the teacher's delivery context, these exercises might be more guided or flexible according to the needs of the students. In a guided scenario, the teacher might spend classroom time to review the scenario and develop the lesson context based on in-depth discussion with the classroom as a whole. A more flexible practicum would be to allow students to work individually or in small groups to review the artifacts during class time and allow them to discuss and ask questions during a Q&A time allocated for the lesson practicum.

A flipped classroom scenario would be to provide the students artifacts and guidelines for the study materials and then during class time, assign students roles within the lesson context and allow them to "act out" and/or participate in an interactive real-world scenario.

In most cases, the more flexibility the students can be offered in a lesson via the practicum, the greater the impact on comprehension and understanding, although this is not a guaranteed outcome. It's possible that some of the small work groups aren't effective at discussing and analyzing the lesson context while other small groups can easily handle the practicum. This could be because a strong leader or a small group of high performers join together in a small group. In cases like these, the teacher must review the small groups and how they were created and organized in order to allow all the groups and individuals to benefit from the practicum.

Critical thinking and collaboration can go hand in hand. The more practical and real-world the lesson and delivery scenario, the more the critical-thinking practicum can be effective. But this is not necessarily always the case. When determining the delivery context and the implementation of artifacts, the teacher must determine the best practicum for the students to exercise the critical-thinking exercises and not let the idea of collaborative groups always be the rule instead of the exception.

6. Collaboration

As mentioned before, collaboration as defined in the lesson and delivery context is the aspect of 6C that can be most managed and/or manipulated by the teacher. Most T4c will be flexible enough to support many delivery contexts that may or may not include a collaboration component. Let's look at different levels of engagement through collaborative exercises. Remember, the idea being that any T4c lesson should be able to be delivered with any of these collaboration models.

It would be impossible to do an exhaustive review of all possible collaboration models. The most salient point of collaboration in T4c or in any curriculum delivery, for that matter, is that learning is still the key. Collaboration to enhance student engagement and comprehension is always good. If scores can demonstrate improved mastery and comprehension over time that's even better.

Table 8.1. Collaboration Models

Collaboration Models	
Small Group 2–3 Students	A small group working together physically, verbally, or on a single collaboration exercise using one device. The device use model could be one student driving or sharing the single device on a shared document. The second scenario could be each student using their own device to collaborate on a single shared document. This scenario doesn't require physical proximity or synchronization—this model could be executed entirely remotely.

Work Group 3–5 Students	Work groups of 3 to 5 students can take on numerous forms:
	    Competing groups working on the same projects
	    Departmental groups working on aspects of a larger project
	    Both on-site and remote models
	    Both synchronous and asynchronous models

Leader-Led	Leader-led groups can be from 5 up to a full class of students. This scenario calls for designated leaders. These were discussed in chapter 3—leadership constructs. In this scenario, the leader can designate multiple students within the group to take on specific roles, such as notetaker, designer, artist, talent, writer, etc.

External Group	External groups include groups external to the classroom group. Examples of these types of collaboration include:
	    Groups from different schools working on the same or competing projects
	    SME groups from educational resources (other schools, universities, and other educational organizations)
	    SME groups from trade or discipline organizations, such as legal organizations, science and mathematics organizations, performing arts, etc.

Whole Class	Collaboration projects that engage the whole class can be easy or overwhelming. It all comes down to organization of the lesson plan and clear direction in the delivery context. Once again, projects that engage with all students in a class can be remote or on-site, synchronous or asynchronous. They may require each student to contribute or for small groups to work together toward a final single deliverable.

POSSIBLE NEGATIVE IMPACTS OF COLLABORATION

Collaboration can also have negative impacts on curriculum and learning. Let's take a moment to understand how these scenarios can be avoided. It becomes incumbent of the teacher over succeeding implementations of lesson delivery to understand which collaboration models offer the highest probability of positive impact on the classroom and their resultant test scores.

Table 8.2. Possible Negative Impacts of Collaboration

Possible Negative Impacts of Collaboration	
Technical Issues	Requiring students to work on a shared document on a specific platform will fall flat unless every student has a device that can access the lesson artifacts equally among all students. If some students don't have the right device or don't have access to Wi-Fi, suddenly the collaboration model turns upside down. Students lacking access either by time or functionality are relegated to manual exercises and even forced into nonparticipation.
Personality/Social Issues	Fear of participation in the classroom practicum can also manifest itself in the online collaboration exercise. Students with poor writing abilities might be hesitant to participate in message boards or exercises where they must write creatively or technically. Students who have had negative experiences online, such as bullying or hazing, might also limit their exposure and risk in collaborative settings.
Personal Issues	Students with severe self-esteem issues might be unable to work with other students or fulfill leadership responsibilities.
Cultural Issues	Students of diverse religions or cultures might inhibit their participation in groups outside their cultural norms. Conversely, an English-fluent student might have difficulty in a majority non–English-speaking class.

TEACHER FUNCTIONAL KNOWLEDGE

Once this pinnacle of T4c implementation is achieved—no one's ever been here before—it's time to discuss the next critical success factor—the teachers!

We stated earlier that the teachers don't need to know the whole 6C development process in order to deliver T4c. They will, however, build familiarity through the review of the 6C survey form accompanying each lesson plan. They will also require a level of technology proficiency. The remaining sections of this chapter will enumerate the requisite skills the teachers must possess to fully implement T4c.

Requisite Skills

DEVICE OPERATING SYSTEM PROFICIENCY

The most obvious aspects of technology proficiency are basic operations of the device and operating system in use by the teachers as well as the students. The teacher must be able to help students with their devices in addition to being adept utilizing the teacher device. It's quite possible the teacher is assigned a Windows laptop for their development, as well as presentation systems, while the students use Android tablets or iPads.

Although this section lists educational and instructional development platforms by name and manufacturer, this list does not attempt to describe any of these platforms in detail as they might go by the wayside in years or even months after this publication.

Whether it's a Windows system, Chromebook, Mac, or Android-based device, the teacher must know the rudimentary basics:

- Device distribution, storage, and charging
- Power on, off, and device power management and proper use
- Access to productivity applications
- Access to Internet web browser
- Device acceptable use policy
- Device ethics and digital citizenship
- Security, penalties, and enforcement

Internet and Resources Search Proficiency

Secondarily, the teacher must know how to access Internet-based resources by accessing and utilizing keyword search functions on the following platforms:

- Google basic and advanced search features
- LMS access to files and search functions
- School/district-based electronic and streaming resources
- Curriculum and instructional warehouse, tools, and resources
- District subscriptions to electronic and streaming video resources

Productivity Application Proficiency

Since it is likely that the first generation of T4c developed out of any development team might be based on MS Office or GAFE platforms, use of the following basic productivity applications in the school/district-based platforms would be necessary:

- Word Processing
- Spreadsheet
- Graphic design and drawing
- Presentation and slides
- Other relevant educational applications

ENHANCED DELIVERY APPLICATIONS

Other presentation or video production applications such as the following might be licensed by the district in order to develop more advance interactive presentations:

- FlowVella
- Keynote
- SlideShare
- Canva
- Keynote
- Prezi

VIDEO PRODUCTION/EDITING

- Adobe Premier
- Corel VideoStudio
- Pinnacle Studio
- Apple iMovie

GRAPHIC DESIGN APPLICATIONS

- Adobe Illustrator
- Adobe Photoshop
- Canva
- CorelDRAW

LEARNING MANAGEMENT SYSTEMS

- Google Classroom
- Blackboard Learn
- Schoology
- Canvas
- Edmodo

VIDEO CONFERENCING APPLICATION

- Zoom
- TrueConf
- Freeconference.com
- GoToMeeting
- Skype Premium

COLLABORATION APPLICATIONS

- Asana
- Basecamp
- G Suite
- MS Team 5
- Slack
- Trello

PROFESSIONAL DEVELOPMENT

We discussed how the teachers are the critical success factor of true T4c. Reminding ourselves that the objective of developing T4c is not about the technology, but it's also not about the curriculum itself. It's about the improvement and effectiveness of teaching; it's a multitiered endeavor.

Yes, the four development tiers of the substitution, augmentation, modification, and redefinition (SAMR) model have now been disrupted, but there's still a development effort ahead. It's the aspect that will truly need to scale to the Nth degree in order for the promise of T4c to be realized. This is the need to bring all teachers up to speed on the T4c concept and to impact their delivery of curriculum in the first implementation after training. And maybe the T4c being developed can become so well packaged and defined that there is no additional professional development (PD) required beyond the basic concepts and training in planning and implementation.

Of course, the issue we're discussing now assumes that your district has done the first step of this developmental cycle by staffing a T4c development team and implementing the platform for the clearinghouse and sharing of the artifacts. As stated in earlier chapters, the PD required for development of T4c must be constant and dynamic. Platforms and curriculum are ever-changing, and just as curriculum is dynamic today in its variety of forms, a district that takes on the responsibility of developing T4c curriculum will also be in a constant state of improvement and endless upgrading and developing. And that's all good!

The better news is that teaching PD for T4c should not be a constant cycle of ever-changing curriculum and artifacts. Once developed according to the state and district standards, the curriculum should be fairly fixed for the near- to midterm. And with the flexibility built into T4c by its nature, teachers should have few issues with keeping the lesson and delivery of the curriculum topical and relevant.

To support the teachers, a scalable model of initial training and ongoing training must be adopted and implemented at the district level. Just as the district instructional services department had to organize and facilitate staffing for development, they also must staff and budget the PD of the T4c.

Following are examples of PD models. Notably, none of them will seem new. Even though the subject matter of T4c is new, the models to support PD remain fairly well defined, and individual schools will have history to determine what PD models have succeeded (or failed) in the past.

District Instructional Resource

It's easy to imagine that the district instructional services department already has resources dedicated to PD, but new questions arise:

IS THE DEVELOPMENT TEAM ALSO TASKED WITH TRAINING AND/OR PROFESSIONAL DEVELOPMENT?

Now that this team is assembled and working, how are they tasked with becoming trainers? Does this even make sense? On the one hand, no. Why would you make an instructional designer, project manager, or curriculum subject matter expert (SME) also a trainer? Well, actually, it does make sense; first, who better understands the concept of T4c and the 6C development process than the development team?

DOES T4C PD REQUIRE A DEDICATED TRAINING TEAM?

Maybe in the biggest district this may be warranted, but most districts already have some sort of leverage model for training and PD. There's no sense in reinventing the PD wheel. If anything, once the initial training regarding the fundamental concepts of T4c are established, the leveraged training model like those discussed below should be sufficient to support expansion and the proliferation of use throughout the district.

DOES T4C REQUIRE DEDICATED TRAINING MATERIALS?

We believe that the 6C survey form, when completed with enough detail to facilitate development of the artifacts and materials, should be enough to support self-paced training.

HOW MUCH PD TIME IS REQUIRED FOR EACH TEACHER?

Once again, the whole concept behind T4c is to create artifacts that leverage the use of technology that is ubiquitous at the site. Along with 6C survey form serving as the training document, teachers should be able to ingest the survey form, inspect the artifacts, and spend an average amount of planning time at the beginning of the week to prepare for delivery of T4c.

Train the Trainer (TtT)

The TtT model has been widely used in industry to facilitate large-scale training without spending egregious amounts of time and money on formal trainers and scheduled training events. By leveraging all members of a district development team and identifying site- and grade-level staff who can take on these additional training scopes, this model can be an effective PD model without engaging or dedicating resources to become full-time trainers and having teachers wait until that annual in-service event where they are blasted with a whole year's worth of training in one day.

This model might have a single district resource (or team of district resources) designated to train a group of teacher-trainers. The focus of the training becomes twofold: (1) to train the teacher-trainers on the T4c and 6C survey form process; and (2) secondarily train them to train site-based teachers.

The trainer resources might be assigned sites and/or grade-level cohorts, who then are designated trainers at the site and to grade-level teachers. These site- and/or grade-level teacher-trainers are then tasked to meet with more granular teacher groups to pass on the training.

Coach/Mentor

The coach/mentor PD model differs from the TtT model in as much as the relationship between coach and mentor becomes a longer-term commitment and dedication between the coach and mentor compel deeper engagement. Just as the models suggest, a TtT model could have ratios of one district trainer acting as the trainer for multiple designated teacher trainers at each site. Just as the TtT model suggests that a single trainer trains a number of teacher-trainers, who in turn train more teachers in a pyramid-style expansion.

The coach/mentor model can be seen as a deeper TtT model in that the coaches will receive some in-depth T4c indoctrination that empowers them to coach a select few mentors during the session or school year. This dedicated assignment could facilitate greater understanding and utilization of the T4c artifacts and lessons.

Standards and Approval Committee

Finally, one of the control features of any project management method is the quality assurance (QA) plan. In normal project management parlance, QA refers to the methods and practices that ensure quality in the planning of an execution process. Whereas a quality control (QC) process is a verification and validation testing of the output or by-product of the process.

So, what is the quality assurance process for your districts' T4c development process? First of all, using a project management methodology like MAPIT® (see the author's previous books) provides a deep dive discussion of quality assurance in a project management process. These are the standards discussed ad nauseum earlier in the book.

We did specify that the standards are part of the QA process, but that's exactly what the MAPIT® process does—secondly is a review or approval committee. This committee might be the T4c development team as a whole, but it might be best to include some regular classroom teachers or site-based resources who have a vested interest in the roll-out of the highest quality T4c. Ultimately the first teachers to get their hands on new T4c curriculum will provide the frontline review process for any by-product, and it will be brutally honest. But any development team is advised to put as much QA process in the defined methodology before it gets in front of any of the trainers, coaches, or teachers.

CHAPTER 8—ACTION ITEMS

1. *Build and Train Your T4c Development Team*

    Now that the team is identified, organized, and resourced, they need a plan. Like any planning process, start with a *mission* and *objectives*.

    The mission is broad-based and for the long-term. The objectives should be for the first cycle, session, or school year.

    Support their efforts with training in the platforms they identify for pilot standards.

    Train the program manager (champion) in project management methodologies to ensure progress to plan, and quality assured deliverables.

2. *Roll Out a PD Model*

    Identify the PD model for your T4c development team to rollout their lessons.

MOVING FORWARD

Now what? It was quite a journey, not unlike a trip to Mars where there was no idea or concept of what to expect. But in summary let's take a quick look at the roadmap laid out so you the educator can take the next logical step and jump straight to T4c development.

Chapter 1, "Disrupting Education Technology," discussed the fundamentals of education technology including where it gets its vision and where this vision might come from within the district. A light discussion of Dr. Ruben Puentedura's SAMR construct provides the basis for improving curriculum using technology. But this process has proved to be daunting if not a recipe for doing nothing. Why you ask? Because the SAMR model in-and-of-itself is not a roadmap to travel to the top, it is a challenge to be accepted and a puzzle to be solved. But how and by whom? It's a little presumptive to propose that this has been completely done for you. Disruption is the key! The question now becomes, how will you disrupt the status quo within your school or district.

Chapter 2, "Instructional and Technological Innovation Strategy," discussed all levels and aspects of the SAMR model in order to map out the improvement cycle. A discourse of how instructional innovation and technology innovation pose two fronts for advancement. But this section also introduced the *line of discontent*, a sort of purgatory for IT and ed tech services where dysfunction and dissatisfaction abound. Be sure that your district moves beyond the line of discontent in your effort to innovate.

Chapter 3, "Key Technology Systems/Features," laid down the functional and practical features that were identified to provide the highest level of technology to curriculum. These systems/features must be implemented as infrastructure in order to move into the realm at the top of the SAMR model. Chapter 3 also discussed the need for a new set of standards. Standards that dictate the formats, user interfaces, color palettes, and layouts for your school's T4c.

Chapter 4, "A New Name for Redefinition," first introduced the 6C concept and how this process provides a structured approach to the design of T4c. The chapter also introduced a variety of development resources that might comprise a T4c development team.

Chapter 5, "The 6C Development Process," provided a more in-depth look at each of the 6Cs and how they impact the planning and development of T4c. A sample of a T4c survey form that can easily be adapted for your school/district was provided.

Chapter 6, "What's after the 6Cs?" dealt with the fact that the 6C process only aids in defining and developing T4c. There are at least three more phases to having a complete, soup-to-nuts lesson plan offering. Implementation of T4c discusses the flexibility inherent in T4c that allows the teacher to ultimately control and customize how the lesson is delivered according to various factors such as the proficiency, mastery, or leadership capacity of the students.

This chapter also brought the reader to the tipping point for planning for the T4c development team structure and implementation plan. This is not an inconsequential undertaking. There will be some education leaders that may have to stop at this point because they cannot engage or commit resources to a pilot initiative. This is truly where the rubber meets the road, as they say.

In Chapter 7, "Disrupting Incremental Innovation," the discussion got into the implementation aspect of T4c and what it might take to actually get a T4c development initiative started in your district. The section illustrated the concept of the *champion*, the skills he or she should possess and how this champion may be the key to kicking off a successful T4c development initiative.

Chapter 8, "Full-Scale T4c Deployment," provided more insight into full-scale deployment of T4c and what skills are required by the implementers and teachers as well as possible bumps in the implementation road. This chapter also provided ideas for PD, which becomes a critical success factor for a true rollout of T4c in your school district.

At this point, what is next is entirely up to you—Champion!

References

Christensen, Clayton M. *Disrupting Class*. New York: McGraw-Hill Education, 2017.
Holtthink. "Interview with David Thornburg, Author of *From the Campfire to the Holodeck: Creating Engaging and Powerful 21st Century Learning Environments*." 2014. Available at http://holtthink.tumblr.com/post/76595159826/interview-with-david-thornburg-author-of-from-the.
Thornburg, David. *From the Campfire to the Holodeck*. San Francisco, CA: Jossey-Bass, 2013.
Vidal, Darryl. *Fail to Plan, Plan to Fail*. Lanham, MD: Rowman & Littlefield, 2017.
———. *Project Management in the Ed Tech Era: How to Successfully Plan and Manage Your School's Next Innovation*. Lanham, MD: Rowman & Littlefield, 2018.
Vidal, Darryl, and Michael Casey. *Vision: The First Critical Step in Developing a Strategy for Education Technology*. Lanham, MD: Rowman & Littlefield, 2014.
Vidal, Darryl, and Michael Casey. *N3XT Practices: An Executive Guide for Education Decision Makers*. Lanham, MD: Rowman & Littlefield Education, 2014.

About the Author

Darryl Vidal has been involved with technology and education all his adult life. Starting in aerospace telecommunications, he worked as a systems engineer for Apple Computer in the late 1980s and began working directly with K–12 schools. By 1994 Darryl began providing technology consulting services to the San Diego Unified School District and many other districts in the region, helping design and implement digital classrooms, wide area networks, VoIP, and wireless campuses. He holds a bachelor's degree in business and a master's in education technology.

For over twenty years, Darryl has been working at the forefront of education technology modernization programs from virtual classroom technology through learning management systems, helping to plan and manage school technology upgrades totaling over $500 million.

BOOKS

Vidal, Darryl, and Michael Casey. *Next Practices: An Executive Guide for Education Decision Makers*. Lanham, MD: Rowman & Littlefield Education, 2014.

Vidal, Darryl, and Michael Casey. *Vision: The First Critical Step in Developing a Strategy for Education Technology*. Lanham, MD: Rowman & Littlefield, 2014.

Vidal, Darryl. *Confucius in the Technology Realm—A Philosophical Approach to Your School's Ed Tech Goals*. Lanham, MD: Rowman & Littlefield, 2015.

Vidal, Darryl. *Fail to Plan, Plan to Fail: How to Create Your School's Education Technology Strategic Plan*. Lanham, MD: Rowman & Littlefield, 2017.

OTHER WORKS

Vidal, Darryl. *Net Dude*. Pittsburgh, PA: Dorrance Publishing, 2003.

Vidal, Darryl, and Marty Harrell. *Backstage: Behind the Curtains with the Greatest Entertainers of the 20th Century*. N.p. 2017.

www.ingramcontent.com/pod-product-compliance
Lightning Source LLC
Chambersburg PA
CBHW051813230426
43672CB00012B/2720